This book is just amazing! It is a life-changing experience to read—one of the best I have ever read. I have bought many copies to give to my children and friends. It has had an impact on everyone who reads it.

ANN MITCHELL
Front Royal, Virginia
Online Reviewer

Charlene Curry is a woman of integrity, wisdom and grace. Her life as a military spouse of a rising army officer and a mother of four active children has been an amazing example of raw stamina, enormous flexibility, and incredible faith in God's sovereignty, love and power.

In *The General's Lady*, Charlene Curry shares the realities of marriage beyond the blissful wedding day. Young wives would be wise to prepare themselves for their hopeful futures by engaging with one trailblazer, Charlene Curry, who paid the price and reaped the rewards.

LILLIAN GASKILL
Co-author with Charlene Gregg of
Fort Lee in Transition: 1940s–1970s:
   Black Quartermaster Officers' Families at Fort Lee, Virginia

I first met Charlene when she and her husband, Jerry, were having Bible Study and prayer meetings in their home in Mannheim, Germany in the early 1970s. What prayer meetings they were! Lives were changed forever.

REV. CHARLENE AMMERMAN
Deputy Director, Chaplaincy, Full Gospel Churches
and author of *After the Storm*.

I have known Charlene for over 30 years. Her life is full of the light of Jesus. She is the "sweet fragrance of Christ" that draws many to Jesus. As the General's wife and beyond, she leads with the love of Jesus . . . and others follow.

JILL WIEGAND,
wife of the late Army General Robert Wiegand.

The GENERAL'S Lady

The GENERAL'S Lady

GOD'S FAITHFULNESS TO A MILITARY SPOUSE

Charlene Curry

with Irene Burk Harrell

BELIEVE BOOKS
Life Stories That Inspire
WASHINGTON, D.C.

The General's Lady

By Charlene Curry and Irene Burk Harrell

ISBN: 0-9787428-7-7
Library of Congress Control Number: 2006933286

Unless otherwise noted, all Scripture quotations are from the *Holy Bible, King James Version.*

Scripture quotations identified as NIV are taken from the *New International Version of the Bible,* © 1984, published by Zondervan. Used by permission. All rights reserved.

Scripture quotations identified as NLT are *The New Living Translation of the Bible,* © 2000, published by Tyndale House. Used by permission. All rights reserved.

"In the Garden," which appears in Chapter 12, was composed by C. Austin Miles, Copyright 1912, copyright renewed 1940 by Rodhaver Company, (no longer in print)

Cover design: *Jack Kotowicz, Washington, DC, VelocityDesignGroup.com*
Layout design: *Annie Kotowicz*

With thanks to Annie Kotowicz for her assistance in the editing process.

Believe Books publishes the inspirational life stories of extraordinary believers in God from around the world. Requests for information should be addressed to **Believe Books** at www.believebooks.com. **Believe Books** is a registered trade name of **Believe Books, LLC** of Washington, DC.

An earlier version of *The General's Lady* was published by Tyndale House Publishers, Inc. in November,1981. All rights to that edition and to the current work now belong to Charlene Curry.

Printed in the United States of America

CONTENTS

1

Two Kids

Down through the winter sunshine snowflakes came,
All shimmering like to silver butterflies
They seemed to whisper softly thy dear name,
And melted with the teardrops from mine eyes.

Once upon a time, Jerry Ralph Curry and I were two little kids living, playing, and growing up in McKeesport, Pennsylvania—singing that song. My young alto blended easily with the other voices in the junior choir of Bethlehem Baptist Church, especially well, I thought, with Jerry's baritone. The sound drifted out through the open church windows and carried across the worn brick of Sunday-quiet Walnut Street. Passersby involuntarily cocked their heads and listened.

Standing in the choir loft in my freshly pressed black robe with its sparkling white stole, I carefully held before me the crisp pages of sheet music. Singing about snowflakes seemed funny when half the congregation was fanning away with wood-handled cardboard fans snatched from the hymn racks on the backs of the long, highly polished oak pews.

I liked the song though, and decided that maybe our choir director—tall, slim, lovable, no-nonsense Mrs. Gertrude Johnson, an opera singer who, it seemed to me, knew more about music than anyone else in the whole world—had chosen it deliberately to help the congregation think cool thoughts.

Glancing for a moment away from her talented, rhythmic hands that were trying to draw words and melody out of the depths of our hearts and voices, my eyes surveyed the fashionably dressed congregation that comfortably filled the high-ceilinged sanctuary.

Most of the women wore the traditional white or pastel pretty gloves and flower-bedecked straw hats that made their ritual appearance with the new spring suits and dresses each Easter. The black patent leather Mary Jane slippers my father had bought me to wear with my new ruffled yellow nylon dress and matching hair ribbon were barely scuffed.

But I knew they would be worn out long before September came. Back then, Labor Day decreed that fall clothes were in order, no matter how much the temperature soared. High fashion was an important part of life as were courtesy, dignity, decency, civility, respect, four-letter-word-free conversations, married parents and good manners. Unfortunately, today we seem to have discarded those cornerstones of my early life. I miss them terribly.

"Your shoes always wear out too soon," my father often said.

We both knew it was my fault, for whenever I heard music— even when it was only down inside me where no one else could hear it—for some reason I got an irresistible urge to spring up onto the tops of my toes and dance. Through the years I'd had many a spanking for ruining my shoes on the way to and from school, by too much dancing on my toes on the rough concrete sidewalks.

A few weeks before school started, Dad took me to his coal mine's Company Store in Elizabeth, for Dad was by profession a coal miner. Ever since I could remember, he had bought me a dozen new dresses before the first bell rang ushering in each new school year.

Now that I was about to enter the sixth grade, I hoped I could talk him into buying me skirts and sweaters. That's what all the big girls wore to Shaw Avenue Junior High, along with their grubby saddle shoes and rolled-down bobby socks.

No, on second thought, I wouldn't mention it but would prime my mother to suggest the change instead. She had much better success than I in talking my father into new things. From much experience I had learned that I fared better with him when I kept quiet and let her take the lead.

Charles Walter Cooper, my father, worked as a motorman in the bituminous mines of the Pittsburgh Coal Company in Sutersville, about twelve miles across the river from McKeesport. It was a steady, well-paying job, and he was highly respected by his fellow employees and employers—so much so that he was fully employed throughout the years of the Great Depression, years when many other working men were desperately searching for any kind of work that would enable them to provide for their families.

My father was opposed to his family's living in a mining town, feeling that the atmosphere there was not conducive to good family life. He believed there would be more advantages available to his children away from the mining town setting. So, for our sakes, he didn't mind getting up extra early in the morning to pack his lunch and drive the long distance to the mine every day.

Deep inside I knew my Dad was a good man, even though he was far too strict in his ways to suit me. It seemed that he was always telling me to be "seen and not heard," to finish my homework, and to do my chores. He also often made me go to bed much too early for my liking.

Perhaps his being such a strict disciplinarian was due to the fact that his mother died from pneumonia when he was fifteen. Dad was the oldest of five children, so it naturally fell on him to help discipline and rear his three sisters—Jessie, Sadie and Gussie, plus his brother, George.

If he overheard me asking Mom a question in a tone of voice he didn't consider respectful or even if I too strongly expressed an opinion contrary to hers, he often interpreted it as "sassing." Then off came his heavy miner's belt and he would deliver several swift strokes across my backside and the calves of my legs.

"You're not going to talk back to your mother!" he'd shout.

Many times there would be tears in his eyes as well as in mine as he labored to "bring up a child in the way she should go." It seemed to only make matters worse if I protested my innocence. Such talk was condemned as "arguing."

Usually I suffered my lashes in silence. Afterward, Dad would sometimes lecture me about how important it was for me to honor my father and mother. Still, I did not see how expressing an honest opinion showed a lack of respect for him or for Mom. And though I sometimes felt his actions were irrational, I still respected and honored him. Children should honor their parents, even when they don't agree with them.

There were times, in the middle of a parental lecture concerning my respect for Mom, that a softer spirit would come over him, and with pain in his voice he would reminisce, telling me what a gracious lady his mother had been, a woman with marvelous hair so long she could sit on it. He loved her with a passion. Her loss had had a profound effect on him that colored the way he responded to things throughout his entire life.

My brother George and I learned early on to keep our mischievous sibling rivalry under cover. From the beginning, Dad had made a rule that if either of us tattled on the other, about anything, he wouldn't waste time in trying to find out who was at fault. He would simply punish us both to make sure he got the right one.

That usually gave me the best end of the bargain, because I pestered George, who was three years younger than I, far more than he ever bothered me.

As my eyes continued to rove over the congregation, I could see George, who was then nine years old, sitting beside Mom, who was so pretty and slim that people often thought she was my sister instead of my mother.

My father was sitting next to the aisle on the opposite side of the church, as the men did in those days, although he didn't always come to church with us.

"A man doesn't prove that he's a Christian by being in a certain place at a certain time," he used to rationalize whenever some church officer got up the courage to question him about his frequent absences.

I suspected the real reason that he stayed at home was that he liked to be using his hands working in the kitchen better than he liked sitting somewhere being idle. As a little girl, I hoped God accepted that explanation as well as I did, and didn't hold it against him.

After the choir had sung its anthem and sat down, the sermon followed. When it was over, the deacons respectfully rose from their pew at the front of the sanctuary. All of them wore dark suits, white-white shirts and black ties, in keeping with the formality of the service.

Before serving communion at the pews, they put on white gloves, as was customary in the Baptist Church we attended.

It was explained to me that this was a mark of reverence for the body and blood of our Lord as they prepared to distribute the gleaming silver trays holding the mysterious elements of the Lord's Supper.

When the communion tray reached me, I lifted one of the tiny cups of grape juice from its place, and then passed the tray to the girl sitting beside me, using that as a good excuse to sneak a glance at handsome young Jerry Curry, sitting directly behind me.

I'd known Jerry for more than two years now, and my heart still sped up when his keen, kind, hazel eyes met mine. I'd been deliciously aware of his clear boyish baritone blending with my deepening alto almost as one voice as we had sung about the winter snowflakes, rejoicing in the wonders of God's creation.

To me, Jerry was one of the most marvelous wonders of that creation. We'd met on a spring Saturday when he was thirteen and I was ten.

2

Charlene Loves Jerry

My father had driven Mom, George, and me from our tall, narrow, now non-existent three-story townhouse on brick-sidewalked Locust Street, past Bethlehem Baptist Church, and across the skeletal steel-trussed 15th Street Bridge which crossed over the Monongahela River. The river was muddied brown by waste from steel plants.

We rode through the few short miles of sparsely populated rural area, then down a rutty, dusty country road, elegantly named Washington Boulevard, located in the McKeesport suburb of Liberty Borough. There, Daddy turned to the right into the steep, short, graveled driveway running up beside the welcoming red brick home of the Jesse Aaron Curry family.

Dad had met Jesse at Bethlehem Baptist Church on one of Jesse's rare visits there. Wiry, brown, jack-of-all-trades, Jesse Curry had invited my father, Charley Cooper, to plant a garden.

"Plenty of room for your family to garden on my place," he'd said. "Get yourself some seeds and come on out some Saturday. I'll be glad to help you break up the land."

And so we had gone with four fresh-cut wooden stobs to mark the corners of the plot, and a ball of string to tie on the turpentine smelling wood to make a straight edge for the rows to follow.

There were packets of seeds in the brown cardboard box sitting between George and me on the back seat of our yellow Oldsmobile. The colorful seed envelopes promised a mouth-watering harvest of radishes, onions, corn, green and lima beans, lettuce, cabbage, carrots, and garden peas. Lying on the floor of the car was a handful of green pepper and tomato plants ready to be set out, their fragile roots wrapped in wet newspaper and tucked into a brown paper grocery bag.

George and I got acquainted with the older Curry boys while the grown-up Coopers visited the grown-up Currys, talking of gardens and politics, labor unions and the price of bricks, Sheetrock and lumber. Mr. Curry and Dad were both skilled handymen, always building something.

The oldest of the Curry boys, named Jesse after his father, was to die in the Army of spinal meningitis a few years later. But on that day, Jesse, along with Jerry and the youngest brother, Bob, raced us to the grassy knoll behind the house. There we played tag, ran barefoot through the cool patches of velvety moss, climbed trees and drank iron-tasting water from the pump over the deep well. Then we peeped into the mysterious mine in the side of the hill where the Currys dug their own coal, marveled at the pink pigs, listened to the baaing milk goats, and then chased the flocks of ducks and chickens that furnished feather pillows, breakfast eggs, and Sunday dinners for the Currys and their paying customers. It was a wonderful idyllic afternoon.

Before the sun went down, the grown-ups had plowed the soil and planted a garden with their hands, and solved the problems of the nation and the world with their words. Meanwhile, George and I had made new friends who were to be a great influence in our lives.

As for me, I had fallen head over heels in love with Jerry Curry. "Puppy love" it was called in those days, but from the beginning, in spite of my youth and immaturity, I knew that this my first love was real and that it would last forever.

Riding home in the back seat of the car, I was so excited that I had to confide in someone. After all, falling in love wasn't the kind of thing a 10-year-old girl did every day. I didn't dare share this monumental experience with my parents, so I bared my heart to George, who was sitting beside me.

"I really love that Bob Curry," I whispered, keeping my voice low so Dad and Mom couldn't hear me above the sound of the engine and scold me for what they would call nonsensical talk.

My heart was pounding so hard, I even got Jerry's name mixed up with that of his younger brother, but George knew who I meant, all right. "I just can't help loving him," I sighed.

George's eyes lit up with a kind of fiendish glee. Too late, I realized I had made a terrible mistake in confiding in him.

"Oh, boy! I'm gonna tell on you!" he tossed back at me, and I knew I was in for it. I was so love-struck I'd been momentarily oblivious of the fact that George and I invariably had a feud going on about something.

I'd unintentionally given him a perfect weapon to use to get even with me for my most recent offense against him. It had been a whopper, and it came thudding back into my memory.

A few days earlier I had poured boiling-hot water out of the kitchen teakettle into George's boot—with his foot in it—when I had asked him to get out of my way and he hadn't moved fast enough to suit me.

The scalding had been painful, but George had been afraid to tell on me because he wanted to avoid contact with Dad's belt. Since George had kept his mouth shut, I'd gotten off scot-free. But now I would have to pay dearly—unless I could talk him out of it.

"Please, George, please don't tell anybody. If you do, I'll never tell you anything else—no more secrets ever again, as long as I live. Please, George?"

It was hard to threaten and plead in soft, whispered tones. Fortunately, Mom and Dad were engrossed in a conversation of their own.

"What'll you give me?" George asked, opening a door for bargaining. In a few minutes' time, he had talked me out of some of my most treasured possessions. Later that night, when the transaction was about to be completed, I was tempted to make him sign his name in blood, but settled for a verbal agreement.

"Now, promise you won't tell," I demanded. "Promise you'll never tell? On your honor?"

"I promise."

He was too glib to suit me, his grin far too wide.

"Please, George. No fair crossing your fingers behind your back."

He stuck his hands out in front of him. "I'm not crossing my fingers. I really promise."

"Cross your heart and hope to die?" I asked him to repeat the ancient formula that insured truthfulness.

"Cross my heart"—he made a wide X across the middle of his chest—"and hope to die." He let his tongue hang out of the corner of his mouth and pretended to keel over in a dead faint.

"You're not tricking me? You really mean it?" I had to be sure it was all legal.

"Naw, I wasn't tricking you. Now give me my stuff."

"Well, all right then. But remember, you promised, and you crossed your heart."

I loaded him down with the things he wanted—my red yo-yo, an old tennis ball, my collection of bubble gum baseball cards, and an almost new Chinese Checker game—and the deal was settled.

George was so nice to me the rest of the week that by the time Saturday rolled around again, I had forgotten there had been a problem between us that is except for the usual secret wrangles without which life could hardly be expected to go on—like whose turn it was to wash the dishes, or sweep the steps, who had tracked mud in on the carpet and should clean it up before Dad found out, whose fault it was that the water had been left running in the kitchen sink, and who got to read the newspaper comic pages first.

But when we next motored out to the Currys, the minute Dad was out of earshot and the Curry boys had come outside to play with us, George cupped his hands to his mouth, made a megaphone and started hollering at the top of his lungs:

"Char-lene lo-oves Jer-ry, Char-lene lo-oves Jer-ry, Char-lene lo-oves Jer-ry . . ."

He went on and on in the singsongy way that must date back to the Book of Genesis. I was so angry at George I could have crowned him with my fist. I felt my face turning almost purple with embarrassment as tears of frustration and rage welled up in my eyes and threatened to spill over.

But suddenly it wasn't so bad, because Jerry seemed to understand—and to be pleased with the announcement. He grabbed my hand and pulled me along with him as we sped to the leafy spring woods over the brow of the hill and beyond the coal pit. There we scrambled, panting, high up into a tree to hide until George had put his mind on something else. I must have put my mind on something else too because I don't ever recall getting even with George for his treachery or even making him give my treasures back to me. Somehow a truce had settled between us. By the end of the summer, Jerry and I were discussing marriage.

Weeks turned into months, then into years, and there were repeated journeyings of the Coopers to visit the Currys, making some of the happiest memories of my childhood. My parents hoed and weeded and harvested their green-topped spring onions, pungent green peppers, and cheery, cherry-red globes of tomatoes in the early summer, pulling mouth-watering ears of sweet corn a little later, and digging Irish potatoes in the fall.

They laid the rich produce on thick layers of clean newspaper for careful wrapping and tying with string into bundles to put into the trunk of the car. That way nothing was bruised on the twenty-minute trip from the farm back to our concrete and cobblestone world.

As the years passed, Jerry and I often discussed marriage and became absolutely certain that his destiny and mine were inextricably linked together for some mysterious high calling that only God knew.

3

Mingled Flavors

Remember now thy Creator in the days of thy youth,
while the evil days come not, nor the years draw nigh,
when thou shalt say, I have no pleasure in them . . .
—Ecclesiastes 12:1, KJV

Before Sunday school, on the morning when the junior choir sang about snowflakes, I had gone to the kitchen where Mom was pinching off wads of dough to shape into rolls, and Dad was cutting and flouring the chicken for frying in the heavy cast-iron skillet.

Mom had on her black silk Sunday dress with the lace collar, with her hair freshly shampooed and the waves combed carefully into place. A bright calico apron was tied about her slim waist to protect her skirt from flour and splashes.

My parents had shared the kitchen work harmoniously as long as I could remember. Both of them were excellent cooks, making the food as picture-perfect to look at as it was super-delicious to eat. But neither of them had any patience with my desire to work alongside them so I could learn their culinary secrets.

They didn't want a child mixing germs in the food, they told me. But I knew that this was only a convenient rationalization. The truth was they just didn't want to be bothered with teaching me.

Still, I yearned to learn how to knead dough and make bread for the family just like they did. Once in a great while, Mom gave in to my pleading, making me scrub my hands nearly to the bone I thought, before she let me punch down the dough for its second rising in the big tan earthenware bowl with the blue bands circling around it. I still make bread using a bowl just like it that my mother gave me when I was newly married.

Sometimes when baking, Mom even gave me a tiny pinch of dough to eat raw before she covered the bulging, yeasty mass with a clean, freshly ironed dishtowel. Then she would set it aside to double in bulk again before shaping it into huge pans of big, flat rolls fit for a king.

Occasionally she would squeeze off a portion of the dough and roll it out very thin, drizzle it with melted butter, sprinkle on generous amounts of sugar and cinnamon, and roll it snugly for slicing into thick rounds that made the most delicious cinnamon rolls this side of heaven.

A few dozen times in my life, when I'd been extra good about something for a change, and when I remembered not to bother her for it ahead of time, Mom had given me a small ball of fluffy dough after it had risen three times and was almost ready to bake.

I patted out the dough, and fried it in a little bubbling lard in the hot skillet on the gas stove. When the bread was crusty brown on both sides, I blotted it on a piece of paper toweling and let it cool a little before slathering it with grape jelly.

Somewhere I'd read about the ambrosia and nectar of the gods in ancient Greece and intuitively knew those things couldn't possibly be as good as my mother's yeast bread or my father's succulent southern fried chicken and incomparable potato salad.

These were good years. World War II was over, peace reached around the globe. There was plenty of work for those who wanted it and salaries were high. McKeesport was a rich, growing city. Life seemed to bubble up all around.

"Mom," I asked when she looked up from her work that particular Sunday morning, "in case Jerry Curry asks me to go with him for ice cream after church, is it all right with you for me to go, please?"

I got right to the point, but very politely, so Dad wouldn't have any reason to think I was haranguing mother, being disrespectful toward her or "running my mouth" unnecessarily. Then I waited quietly and patiently for her answer, hardly daring to breathe for fear she'd say no or Dad would lay down some kind of negative edict, one irrevocable for eternity.

"I guess so," she said finally, looking at me thoughtfully. Then, half scolding, she warned, "But don't take too long at it. Come straight home afterward. You know your father won't like it if you're late for dinner. And don't eat so much ice cream that you spoil your appetite. Remember, we'll be going to Elizabeth to see your grandmother this afternoon."

I was glad when the list of prohibitions was finished. I loved to go see grandmother and grandfather, whom we called Mum and Pup, when their red and pink and white peonies and apple and cherry trees were in bloom. But the blossoms were gone now, and it was too soon to pick cherries.

With no other children to play with in Mum and Pup's neighborhood, George and I found the visits sometimes rather boring. Elizabeth was eight miles on the other side of the river, and this was a Sunday when I would have rather stayed home, but I knew that would never be allowed.

So I said, "Yes, I know," as pleasantly as I could, and thanked Mom for giving me permission to be with Jerry, even if it was for just a little while.

Dad looked up from dredging chicken legs with flour, salt and pepper and gave a little snort of approval or disapproval, I couldn't be sure which—even though I knew he had high regard for Jerry and his hardworking family. Then Dad washed the flour off his hands and reached into his pocket for a little handful of coins so I'd have something for the collection plate.

I thanked him for the money, and off I raced, hoping the sermon wouldn't be too long, and that Jerry would indeed invite me to eat ice cream with him. I wasn't that hungry for ice cream—it was just a good excuse to be with him.

We were too young to date and the minutes we shared at Sunday school, church, choir rehearsal on Thursdays, and gardening on Saturdays were not enough time for us to be together. We both cherished every stolen moment.

After church, when I was hanging my choir robe in the choir room, Jerry walked over to me and looked to the bottom of my soul in that direct way he had, even as a boy.

"Did you ask your mother if we could have ice cream before you go home?"

Happily I nodded my assent.

"Good, let's go then."

He took my hand and we walked together down the church steps, onto the sidewalk, and a few more feet to Jimmy's Restaurant, which nestled close to the side of the church.

Both buildings rose straight from the concrete, with no hint of a lawn. Jimmy's place, with its awning-covered picture windows, invited passersby into a cool interior, where lazy, large-bladed fans turned slowly against the high, ornately baroque-plastered ceiling.

Jerry led me to one of the red-painted booths, where we ordered thick, creamy milkshakes—chocolate for Jerry, vanilla for me. Jerry paid for them with money he earned as a part-time janitor at a local dress shop.

In the precious moments while we waited for the whirring machines behind the marble counter to prepare our shakes, we held hands across the table and drowned in each other's eyes, trying to get enough of looking to last until we would see one another at choir practice after school on Thursday.

To me, Jerry was fantastically good looking, nothing at all like the other boys, though he was of average size and build. Even his clothes looked different—gray knickers, a soft white shirt, and a tweed jacket with a yoke across the back, and a belt attached to the jacket. There was a striped ascot around his neck, completing the out-of-the-ordinary style.

Other boys never wore ascots; if anything they wore bow ties, as if there was a law against any variation from the uniform. To my way of thinking, Jerry's clothing was romantic—it looked more university-European than steel-working, coal-mining Pennsylvanian.

When Jimmy brought our orders, we stopped holding hands long enough to unwrap the fat soda straws, then joined hands again and closed our eyes while Jerry asked God to bless the milkshakes, amen.

In several years of frequenting Jimmy's establishment, I never got to know him, because Jerry and I had eyes only for each other. No one else in the world mattered when we were together. But I can see Jimmy still, a middle-aged, sturdily built man. Around his ample middle was always tied an enormous white apron, brightly colored by stains of every flavor of the rainbow.

If we happened to order banana splits instead of milkshakes, as we did sometimes, shyness and insecurity rose up to plague me. Because I was such a slow eater, the ice cream would melt under the gooey assortment of toppings, threatening to make little rivers across the swirled red formica table.

Hoping he wouldn't notice how messy I was, I'd surreptitiously shove a paper napkin or two under the lip of the ice cream dish to make a little dam to catch the rivers while Jerry shared his heart with me.

There was a strange and wonderful dream he had of living in a beautiful chateau with crystal chandeliers. Whenever Jerry talked about it, I knew it was a dream in which I would play a part.

Such a chateau was a far cry from the little brick home his father had built with his own hands, his young sons helping him mix the mortar and carry bricks, and his wife sewing curtains, painting woodwork, and hanging wallpaper bought with money saved from picking and selling blackberries.

And such a French country house was also a far cry from the tall, narrow townhouse where I lived, a few blocks from where the busy streets of McKeesport gave way to a rocky slope that plunged to busy railroad yards and clanging steel mills and factories lining the banks of the Monongahela River.

That wonderful dream was a long way from our beginnings as the son and daughter of honest, hardworking, blue-collar folks in a small Pennsylvania city. Yet even that was an important part of God's plan for us. And I believed there was more, much more.

The urban neighborhood where I grew up was polyglot, a microcosm of melting-pot America. There were Greeks, Syrians, Italians, Chinese, and some Jewish families from old Germany. At Nick's, the neighborhood grocery store, change was counted out to the local children in Italian.

My own people and Jerry's were of mixed racial and national heritages—red, white, and blue/black, colors as American as the flag itself. The Native American strain was almost a pure-blooded line in part of Jerry's father's family. Jerry's paternal grandmother's portrait hanging on the wall of the house in Liberty looked exactly like the stately, unapproachable wife of a powerful Indian chieftain.

The white strain was strong in my mother's parents, who were both half French, very fair skinned. Their parents had moved down the coast from Canada, bringing their own grapevine cuttings from stock that had been rooted in France. According to an aunt on my father's side of the family, my paternal grandmother was part Jewish, though that was never substantiated.

Jerry had more Irish in him than just his magnificent singing voice. Neither of us could trace our roots back very far, but hoped to some day. Yet the little ancestral tracing Jerry did do, revealed that some of his ancestors were black slaves and black freedmen, while more than a few were white slave owners.

Like many Americans, we are blended from among the major groups of people who make up this great land. As the years went on, God moved us all around the United States and the world, giving us the opportunity to know Germans and Koreans, Californians and Texans, New Englanders and Georgians, Midwesterners and Coloradans, politicians, doctors, engineers, college professors, carpenters, and tenant farmers.

Slowly we came to feel that it wasn't just happenstance that we had lived everywhere, working among all these different kinds of people, with Jerry being in command positions over tens of thousands of men and me serving as the lady at his side. God had planned every detail of our lives.

Looking back, I see that when Jerry and I were just two little children from McKeesport, the things that could happen only in America were already beginning to happen. A unique foundation was being laid.

4

Two Are Better Than One

Jerry graduated from McKeesport High School in June 1950 and went to work alongside his father as a scarfer and welder in the Pittsburgh Steel Foundry. That same month, North Korea invaded South Korea. In early March of 1951, Jerry enlisted in the United States Army as a private along with many other red-blooded eighteen year olds who considered it a privilege to serve their country in wartime.

Although he enlisted to fight in the Korean War, after Basic Training the Army sent him to Germany . . . out of my sight but never out of my mind for a single day. I often heard myself singing to the tune of a then-popular folk song, "He'll come back and marry me, handsome Jerry Curry," and in my youthful innocence and exuberance, I was counting on it.

I was then an eleventh grader at McKeesport High, climbing the 114 steps every morning to the top of the hill where the old beige brick school building overlooked the city with its valley full of factories belching brown, gray and black smoke. Sometimes the sooty snow was so deep, I plodded my way up the slippery hillside without seeing a single one of the creosoted railroad ties which were embedded in the hillside as stair steps.

Jerry was in Germany for a year and then came home . . . just to see me, I wanted to believe. Of course, I'm sure he had also missed his family and wanted to see them. He was nineteen.

Then, just as quickly, he left for Officer Candidate School at Fort Benning, Georgia. He was there for the better part of a year, completing school and being commissioned a Second Lieutenant of Infantry. He stayed at Fort Benning a few months longer to attend Ranger School.

As swiftly as he had left, he returned. It was March of 1953. Suddenly, Lieutenant Jerry Curry was once more visiting his parents and, of course, finding time for me. In fact, on this visit he seemed much more interested in spending time with me than his family. Or was it just my imagination?

The only storm cloud on the horizon was that the Korean War was swiftly building to a climax. I dreaded that I might lose him to it. So I prepared myself for the worst. Many families in McKeesport had already lost loved ones to the war. I prayed daily that if he was sent off to Korea, nothing would happen to him and that he would return to me alive and in one piece.

Once again, he was sitting beside me on the lipstick-red couch in my parents living room. There was a coal fire glowing in the small fireplace—"Just enough to break the chill," Mom said.

Jerry slipped to one knee, took both my hands in his, again looked into the depths of my soul and asked, "Will you marry me?"

The answer to that question had been settled in my heart long ago—forever. I'd made a pledge to God about it, praying, "Lord, if Jerry Curry asks me to marry him, I surely will." Even though I suspected that Jerry would probably leave for Korea shortly after our wedding, I wasn't the least bit hesitant.

But for all my prior planning, the suddenness of his proposal startled me. For a minute I studied the pattern in the oriental rug at my feet, its intricate design overlaid with shadows from the streetlight filtering through the white venetian blinds at the tall front window.

I'd been thinking that we'd probably have a long engagement, at least until he'd finished his military service obligation. That would give me time to go to college for a few years and, at the same time, to continue pursuing my vocal studies. They were coming along quite well and there was the possibility that I might have a concert career.

But Jerry made it plain he wanted to get married now. He was "tired of being a lonely bachelor, living in barracks," he said. And I was afraid I'd lose him forever if I told him I wanted to wait, so I said, "Yes."

Then we talked for a while about what we wanted from life. I really didn't know how to express myself but I knew that Jerry had to be a part of it—whatever I did—or it wouldn't count for anything.

When my father came into the room a little later, Jerry politely stood to his feet and formally asked for my hand in marriage. Their conversation revolved around what were then the classic questions and answers, both of which suddenly became personally significant to me.

"Do you really know what you're doing, young man?"

The question came so sternly from my father that someone less stalwart than Jerry might have been intimidated.

"Daddy, please don't scare him away!" I breathed.

But Jerry was quite undaunted. "I do, Sir. I do," he replied, respectfully, but with calm assurance.

"And just how do you expect to support Charlene—and yourself?"

Again Jerry answered firmly. "Sir, at present, I intend to remain in the U.S. Army, serving my country."

If there were stars in my eyes and a song dancing in my heart amidst the butterflies when Daddy gave his consent, who could blame me? *I could always go to college later*, I told myself.

I graduated from high school on June 2, 1953. Four days later I floated down the carpeted parsonage stairs of Bethlehem Baptist Church. I was wearing a mid-calf, lacy white wedding dress and veil, carrying a small bouquet of yellow roses and fragile baby's breath on top of a white Bible.

Jerry, standing at the foot of the stairs to receive me, caught his breath. His khaki parade uniform was sharply creased, ironed to wrinkle-free perfection, and tucked into brown boots shiny as mirrors. I smiled, knowing he hadn't expected me to be so dressed up.

We had deliberately kept it a small, quiet ceremony because my mother was seven months pregnant with my brother Gary. It was a difficult pregnancy and she was not feeling well. The doctor feared the excitement of a large wedding might cause her to miscarry.

After our pastor had pronounced us man and wife, we dutifully spent time at my parents' home enjoying the joyous wedding reception. It was crowded with too many people and it seemed there was enough food to feed the whole city.

As soon as we could, even before it was quite socially appropriate, Jerry and I sneaked away to be alone.

5

Clearing the Air

The whirlwind months and years that followed, blur into an infinite procession of household moves, endemically necessary in military life, from one end of the world to another. Unpacking and getting almost settled just in time to be uprooted became the norm, as new orders transferred us from one state or continent to another.

It seemed we were constantly saying good-bye to old friends, then greeting strange new faces. In the midst of it all there was always the endless washing, starching, and ironing of uniforms. Each move and every promotion required the sewing on of new patches for each of the ten sets of olive drab fatigues. Every patch had to be perfectly placed, not varying even by a hair's breadth.

Our first duty station was Fort Benning, Georgia, where Jerry attended Airborne School. We didn't see much of each other. Honeymooning and Airborne School didn't mix very well.

Up early each morning, Jerry was off to Fort Benning before daylight. When he returned at dusk, he was dog tired and dragging. But that didn't dampen the excitement of being newlyweds.

Much of my day was spent alone getting acquainted with myself, and trying to adjust to being married and to living in the then-segregated South. These were the days before the Civil Rights Act was passed and there were still signs reading "colored" or "white" prominently screwed into the walls above every public water fountain and restroom.

This overt racial separation and the fact that I was very shy by nature made me slow in getting acquainted with the other military wives. In addition, I was lonely and scared of the late afternoon thundershowers which came up, as they often did, in the oppressive heat. At the first flash of lightning, which always seemed to be aimed at the roof right over my head, I'd go tearing down the steps to place a long-distance phone call to Mom. It was comforting to have someone to talk to during the worst part of the storms but, in retrospect, holding an electrical line in my hand wasn't the smartest thing to do.

At first I had to scrub the uniforms kneeling beside our bathtub, using an old-fashioned washboard and a stiff brush to get them clean. But I soon had enough of that drudgery, even though many wives were doing it without complaint. Just to tease me, Jerry handed me a ten dollar bill one morning and told me to go ahead and buy a washing machine. We really couldn't afford to buy one.

You can imagine his amazement that evening when he came home and found a Sears truck parked outside the apartment and a serviceman inside installing a Kenmore washing machine. To really rub it in, I handed Jerry back five dollars change.

I had gone into town on errands and by good fortune had discovered that Sears was having a special sale on washing machines. The terms were five dollars down and a monthly payment for life, or something like that. Quickly I said, "Yes," signed the papers and Sears guaranteed same day delivery.

All of this was quite a transition for a young girl who had never before been more than fifty miles from home and had never shouldered a single major responsibility.

Jerry did not get to the war in Korea as we had anticipated but was assigned to Fort Campbell, Kentucky—our next stop. It was the home of the 503rd Airborne Infantry Regiment, nicknamed "The Rock" for its heroic parachute assault onto the island of Corregidor when General MacArthur liberated the Philippines. At Campbell we rattled around in a much-too-spacious second-floor apartment made from a converted barracks.

The accommodations were far from homey, until Christmas time when Dad, Mom, brother George, and my new baby brother Gary—born after my wedding—came to spend the holidays with us. What a celebration we had! Daddy had packed the car with enough groceries, it seemed, to provision the whole army. Mom brought along a special earthenware bowl identical to the one she used for making bread and heavy cookie sheets for baking rolls, so everything would "turn out right."

The smell of dough rising in my little kitchen made my first Christmas away from home a real one. I was part of the family again. An added blessing was that all the utensils they brought with them became my very own when they left. Until this day, the large bowl remains one of my prized possessions. It is cracked now, but still serviceable.

Cradling sweet baby brother Gary in my arms made me long to have a baby of my own to hug close to my heart. Jerry wanted a family too, and soon our first baby was a growing bulge under my size eleven dresses.

Pregnancy seemed to banish all my loneliness in a flood of joy and domesticity. Now there was something more than laundry and patches to think about. There was a baby for me to plan for. Feeling greater acceptance of myself than I had ever felt before, I now found it easier to make friends among some of the other military families.

Jerry and I joined with the three other couples in our stairwell for clean-up parties. We would go from apartment to apartment scrubbing all the floors. Then we'd celebrate by going out for steak or spaghetti, knowing that later in the month we'd have to pay for our extravagance by subsisting on canned goods. But even that was fun in our youthful exuberance.

For the most part, life at Fort Campbell was a happy time—at least for the first eight months. It seemed that army life wasn't going to be so bad after all—except for Jerry's parachute jumps. As I saw it, they were far too dangerous.

It was at Campbell under the tutelage of the senior military wives of the 503rd Airborne Infantry Regiment that the social graces and responsibilities expected of officers' wives were indelibly etched into my character.

We had "high teas" and those who officiated or "poured" were always duly mentioned in the local area newspaper. Arriving at a social function in the wrong type dress or failing to wear gloves or a hat, when appropriate, seemed to create a near crisis, or was it a scandal? Silver, china, crystal, candles and flowers were always meticulously placed at table and the subjects of conversations were never allowed to be inappropriate or to give offense.

Though learning social graces is considered by many to be mostly frills, it taught me something far more precious. It taught me the duties and responsibilities of being a First Lady, for the time when my husband would become "the commander," and we would jointly preside over a military community.

I also learned the importance of community service. Through the encouragement of senior wives and commanders, I became involved in all sorts of voluntary programs from helping at the community nursery, to clerking at the base thrift shop, to helping Army Community Service, to being a Red Cross Gray Lady volunteer at the military hospital. These were activities I would continue for the next thirty years.

When Jerry's regiment jumped, I usually stood at the kitchen window of our apartment, my heart in my mouth as I watched the white parachutes floating down toward the landing area. These were the early days of parachuting, not like it is now. Chutes were small and accidents were frequent.

Sometimes a chute would malfunction. Instead of filling with air, it would flap helplessly out of control, like a tablecloth fastened by one corner. When that happened, the chutist's reserve parachute was supposed to take over and correct the malfunction, but sometimes it didn't.

Jerry made his last jump a week before we left Fort Campbell. Three men died during that jump. I was so thankful that in May of 1954, we were ordered to primary flight school at San Marcos, Texas. There Jerry would be landing in his airplane, instead of jumping out of it.

Suitable housing at Gary Airforce Base in San Marcos, Texas was nonexistent. But rather than go home to McKeesport, I chose to stay with Jerry in an apartment that should have been condemned. I was five months pregnant. The flying cockroaches seemed almost as big as the aircraft Jerry was learning to fly, and those cockroaches were the most persistent things in the world.

I exerted most of my efforts—and half of the housekeeping budget—trying to get rid of them. But in two or three days they'd return—with reinforcements. I was beginning to believe that insects would one day take over the world!

Military Flight School was not easy. Over half the officers washed out and were dropped from the flight program. But as with most difficult challenges, Jerry seemed to take it all in stride and had little difficulty successfully completing the course of instruction.

After graduating from the U.S. Air Force's Primary Flight School, Jerry was reassigned to Fort Sill, Oklahoma to attend the Army's advanced flying program.

Leaving the cockroaches behind in midsummer, we drove to Fort Sill for three sweltering months where Jerry learned Army tactical flying, artillery aerial fire adjustment and instrument flying.

In October came a "flying" trip to the hospital for me to give birth to a beautiful baby girl. Jerry named her for me, and called her "Charlein." She would later, as a teenager, take the name of "Charlie" by which she is known to this day.

The timing was perfect. I had a new baby girl to cuddle and two weeks later Jerry had another set of silver wings to pin above his paratrooper insignia over his left shirt pocket. I recall this being a trying time for Jerry when one of the redneck flight instructors tried to wash him out of flight school.

This was a straightforward case of racial bias and prejudice. The instructor had been born and had grown up in the deep south and openly spoke of his disdain for all "Negroes." But through the grace of God, Jerry was able to overcome him and his hatred and still graduate.

So along with a three-week-old baby, we landed at then-drab Fort Riley, in Kansas, the home of the Tenth Infantry Division (Mountain), Jerry's new duty station.

The division was called *mountain* because its soldiers had been specially trained to fight and survive under harsh mountain conditions. The division captured a number of high peaks in the Alps and Apennines during World War II and later fought in Iraq and Afganistan.

I didn't complain about being in Kansas because it was beginning to look like Jerry would entirely miss the Korean War.

A cold, dreary winter set in almost as soon as we turned the key in the door of our apartment in the two-story brick building where heavy snowdrifts kept Charlie and me marooned. The days always seemed too short for all I had to do.

I felt like a robot programmed to get through the demanding sameness of the days—the unending ironing of creases into Jerry's uniforms, breaking my neck in my inherited perfectionistic efforts to keep the apartment as spotless as my mother had always kept her house. And feeding the baby, feeding the baby, feeding the baby . . .

Please don't misunderstand. I loved my baby. It was just a very difficult time. These days mothers have so many more "helps" than we mothers did back then.

Christmas came, but my McKeesport family couldn't come to spend it with us this time. My joy drained away, along with the carefree abandon of honeymoon days. Playing house had been replaced by real life. My stomach ached and my head hurt.

There had been five moves in less than two years, and I wondered if I would ever catch up with myself, put down roots and belong anywhere again. Looking back, I recognize that I had a typical case of post partum blues. No one explained that to me at the time, and Jerry was working too hard to notice that anything was wrong.

Then in the spring of 1955 came big orders—a real uprooting for our first overseas assignment together: Schweinfurt, Germany. True, I wanted to travel, but the thought of a whole ocean between me and my family in McKeesport was terrifying.

As I look back on it now I marvel at how young, naive and immature I was. Nothing in my upbringing had prepared me for the life I was now living. My parents had done their best, but the results weren't much to brag about. The good news, though, was that I was able and determined to learn what it took to be a good citizen, wife, mother, and useful, contributing member of the community.

We were to depart for Germany in June, but first we stopped at McKeesport where Jerry's mother took me aside because she wanted to talk about what she called, "Some very serious and important business."

"Charlene, you're going to be a long way from friends and family now," Mom Curry had said, making the understatement of the year. We sat together at the bright oilcloth-covered table in her kitchen, its deep window sills filled with riotously blooming pink begonias along with lavender and white African violets.

"If you have any problems—and most people have a few now and then," she chuckled, "or if you are afraid about anything, you won't always be able to pick up a phone and call your mother so she can comfort you."

I knew that was true since I had already worried about whether or not there would be thunder and lightning storms in Germany, and how I would cope should baby Charlie become sick with fever and I couldn't call Mom for advice.

"Now, I don't want to meddle in your affairs," Mom Curry went on, her graying hair drawn back to the nape of her neck in a businesslike bun, "but for my own satisfaction, I just need to make sure of something before you go."

Mom Curry was looking straight through me, not accusingly, but in the sweet, smiling way she had even when she was being deadly serious.

"I know my son Jerry has asked the God of Abraham, Isaac and Jacob to take charge of his life," she went on, opening her well-worn Bible on the table before her, "because I was there when it happened. And with my own ears I heard him confess his sins, acknowledge Jesus as his Lord, and invite Him into his heart.

"But all I know about your relationship with God is that you joined Bethlehem Baptist Church when you were about twelve years old. Church membership isn't the same thing as having a personal relationship with the living Lord," she explained, turning the pages of her Bible.

When she found the passage she was looking for, she got right to the point: "Charlene, I don't feel right about letting you go all the way across that ocean without making sure you have the relationship you need so that you can look to God to help you in the stressful situations that are bound to arise."

I swallowed a lump in my throat, being touched that Mom Curry cared enough about me to be thinking of such things.

My memory took me back to the days when I was a child and had wanted to respond to an altar call, in the Baptist tradition, but had been too shy to walk forward.

Then there had come the day when, shy or not, there was no way I could have remained in my pew. I literally had to walk to the church altar and declare Jesus the Lord of my life. I couldn't put it off any longer.

Something real had happened to me that day. Tears had streamed down my cheeks as I made public my desire to be God's child and promised to always live for Him.

When I was baptized on Easter Sunday morning a few weeks later, I came up out of the water knowing that I was a new creature, that I had been truly "born-again"—this time spiritually, not physically.

During the years since then, I had wanted to live for God, but had failed more often than I had succeeded. Trying to live the Christian life was a struggle for me. And even though what I had experienced as a twelve-year-old was real, I thought perhaps repeating my commitment in front of Mom Curry would make a difference.

She asked me if I was willing to pray with her to receive the Lord, so she could know that I was right with God, and I quickly told her I'd be glad to. She showed me some familiar passages of Scripture in Romans 10:8–11 and had me read the ninth verse aloud to her: "That if thou shalt confess with thy mouth the Lord Jesus, and shalt believe in thine heart that God hath raised him from the dead, thou shalt be saved" (KJV).

Following the biblical instructions, I told Mom Curry that Jesus was my Lord and that I believed in my heart that God had raised Him from the dead. According to God's own Word—and God cannot lie—I was saved. It wasn't a matter of opinion. It was a fact.

We prayed and I confessed my sins so they could be forgiven. She had me read 1 John 1:9 aloud to her so I'd know that such a promise was in God's Word.

The whole conversation didn't take more than five minutes, but it accomplished a lot. I got up from the table in the cheery kitchen feeling completely clean, absolutely certain that my relationship with God was on firm ground.

That day I left the house confident that life would be smooth sailing from there on out, thinking that I had everything I needed. In retrospect, I didn't know how naive I was!

6

On Our Way

My help cometh from the LORD, which made heaven
and earth. He will not suffer thy foot to be moved:
he that keepeth thee will not slumber. Behold,
he that keepeth Israel shall neither slumber nor sleep.
—Psalm 121:2–4, KJV

The familiar old song "Sleep my child, and peace attend thee," had comforting words, but no lullaby could put me to sleep. I was too exhilarated and too afraid, excited to be on my first airplane flight and yet fearful of flying across the Atlantic Ocean to Europe.

Along with Jerry, Charlein and I were on the military chartered flight with a planeload of uniformed soldiers and their families from Headquarters Company, 86th Infantry Regiment, Tenth Infantry Division.

Secretly I was very uneasy about flying through the night over all that water! On the one hand I was eager to see the world, but at the same time I was apprehensive about leaving all that was familiar and secure. The Korean War had ended and I thanked God that we were all going to Germany as a family rather than waiting alone while Jerry was fighting that war.

Most everyone on the plane was asleep, Jerry with his head tipped over against the window and eleven-month-old Charlie on the seat between us. I had chosen to sit on the aisle so I wouldn't have to look at the water below.

Above the drone of the engines of the old MAT (Military Air Transport) prop plane, a Lockheed Super G Constellation, I could hear occasional bursts of snoring from other nearby passengers. They seemed to be at peace, but my mind was in turmoil churning with scary questions: *What if we have engine problems? What if we have to land on the water? What if . . . ?*

My anxieties were so great that they finally overcame my natural timidity and propelled me down the aisle toward the cockpit where I intended to check on things. I had just begun to open the door when a flight officer came up behind me and asked where I thought I was going and what I thought I was doing.

"I-I-I just came up to see if everything is okay," I stammered. He must have dealt with frightened, inexperienced passengers before, because he just laughed and let me stick my head into the cockpit for a reassuring look.

Pilot and copilot seemed to be paying attention to what they were doing, their eyes sweeping the instrument panel and the endless horizon unfolding before them.

They smiled in a friendly way at the concern they could read in my eyes, and told me everything was under control, going along quite routinely, perfectly on schedule, no problems, no emergencies anticipated. But if something came up, they would let me know.

Satisfied that they knew their business, and that no emergency red lights were flashing, I thanked them, closed the door softly, walked back to my seat, buckled my seatbelt, yawned, and didn't wake up until we landed in Iceland for refueling.

The next stop was Shannon, Ireland, but no one had told me we'd be stopping there, and when we banked for our approach, hours before our scheduled arrival in Germany, my anxieties revved up to takeoff speed again.

Certain the plane must be having problems, I was ready to get off and stay off. It took some doing, but Jerry finally persuaded me that all was well, and I somehow settled back and survived the rest of the trip.

Disheveled and weary beyond belief, I walked down the steps at Frankfurt-Main Airport, wondering if I could take a ship back when the time came for our return to the United States. For someone who had just renewed her faith in God and His paternal care, I wasn't doing too well.

Our group was met at the airport by a rather unspectacular bus that took us to Schweinfurt, which was to be our home for the next three years, via stops at Aschaffenburg and Wuerzburg. Three years in one place was almost too heavenly to contemplate.

We might actually get all our belongings unpacked in that period of time. How good it would be, for a change, to be "settled," a word I'd all but forgotten.

In a way, we were settled from the first day we arrived. When we walked into our quarters on the second floor of 17 D Maple Street in the middle of the American community at Schweinfurt, we found beds already made up with fresh linens, towels hung in the bathroom, a refrigerator and pantry stocked with enough food for several days, and a delicious dinner prepared and awaiting our arrival.

Moon and Gail McKenzie, our next-door neighbors in the eighteen-family apartment dwelling, had done everything they could to make us feel thoroughly welcome. It was the best demonstration of good neighborliness I would ever see.

The apartment itself was more than I could have wished for—four bedrooms, a large living and dining area, a bath and a half, a perfect kitchen with more cupboards than I could ever fill, and a separate bed and bathroom for a live-in maid.

To my great delight there was even a well equipped laundry room in the basement. A huge picture window in the living area of each apartment had earned the building the nickname, "the fishbowl." But fishbowl or not, it was a place where I could make a home.

It was also the place where God had chosen many circumstances to help accelerate my growing up and to turn me into a mature person in my own right.

One of the first things I had to decide was whether I would follow the crowd and "do as the Romans do," or do what seemed right for me. My natural shyness and formerly entrenched inferiority complex, partly because I hadn't attended college, made it excruciatingly difficult for me to make choices like the other wives seemed to make with no apparent effort. *After all*, I rationalized, *most of them are older than me and far more experienced.* As a result, I was often tempted to do "their thing" instead of making decisions for myself.

The first question that arose concerned how I would spend my time. Most of the other women in our apartment stairwell took advantage of the availability of good, economical household help. Live-in maids were the expected thing, with the money exchange rate a very favorable four marks to a dollar. Having someone else to do their housework and take care of their babies left the women free for all-morning kaffeeklatschs, and all-afternoon bridge parties, and for "doing the town" in the evening.

But although we could have afforded it, initially that lifestyle didn't appeal to me. I saw no sense in hiring anyone to clean house for me when I was strong and enjoyed doing it myself. And I loved taking care of our sweet baby Charlie too much to pay anyone to do that for me.

When I discussed these things with Jerry, he encouraged me to do whatever I really wanted to do, so I took a deep breath and bucked tradition. Instead of spending my mornings in socializing, I chose to dust and clean and polish our quarters as only a perfectionist would.

If others thought I was foolish, I told myself that was their problem. I remained friendly with the other wives without letting them dictate my lifestyle. That independence was a real achievement for me.

As I look back at it now, my decision didn't make a whole lot of sense. But at the time it was important to me because it represented an awakening—something was stirring within me. I was trying to break out of my shy, youthful, inexperienced shell.

Another streak of determination surfaced when army dependents were briefed on what we were to do if we had to evacuate the area under emergency conditions. This was during the Cold War years when Germany lived under the constant threat of a Russian invasion. We lived under the constant threat of a Russian invasion.

The official plan sounded ridiculous to me—wives and children being piled into trucks to escape down the highways. I wrongly figured they would be the first target of the enemy.

In case of attack, I resolved to stay put with the Germans. Such a decision, in retrospect, was not only unwise, but downright stupid. But at the time it served to bolster my confidence in my ability to act independently, a confidence I sorely needed.

More necessities for making decisions of my own arose from the fact that Jerry was often sent on maneuvers to patrol the border between East and West Germany, which was manned by Russians on one side and U.S. soldiers on the other. His assignments sometimes lasted for almost two months, two months when I wouldn't see him and would only occasionally hear from him. To me that presented a fearsome challenge. I needed someone I could depend on, someone who could be counted on to help me. And so for the first time in my life, I prayed a lot.

"O Lord, you've just got to help me. Without you, there's no way I can face today—or tomorrow. Please, Lord. Help me be a good wife for Jerry, and help me properly bring up this darling little girl you have given us."

Then, before many months, there was a new prayer to accompany that one, "Lord help me! Give me strength to cope with the responsibilities of motherhood while I'm having this awful morning sickness." A new baby was on the way.

Things were better when Jerry was not on maneuvers. I didn't feel so all-alone when his homecoming was heralded by the advance arrival of a dozen flaming red roses.

Yet even when in garrison, he was very busy with his job in the daytime, plus spending many night hours taking courses through the extension department of the University of Maryland. He had entered the Army and had become an officer with only a high school education. If he was to compete with his peers he needed a college degree.

Since he worked all day, he could only go to college at night. Fortunately, the University of Maryland and the Army had an agreement whereby the university had opened a series of overseas campuses to provide accredited college courses for military personnel. Without the University of Maryland, Jerry would have had to leave the Army.

It was about then that I learned the wisdom of the older military wives who had quickly welcomed the opportunity to employ inexpensive German house servants. Without the household help it would have been impossible for me to join Jerry in the classroom where I could learn as much of the language and culture of Germany as possible, working toward my own college degree.

Because the servants spoke only German, I had lots of opportunity—and necessity—to practice the German language. I learned enough to enjoy going to German movies. Soon I was shopping or travelling alone, and bargaining with the vendors in the marketplace with no language barrier between us. Even baby Charlie got in the act—she learned her first words in German from our maid, Amy.

Jerry and I became close personal friends with our German teacher, Karl Riederer and wife, Gudrun, who would invite us to their home along with their local German friends. They were instructed not to speak one word of English. We played cards and used every aspect of the game to improve our ability to communicate with our German hosts. Karl was employed by the University of Maryland as part of its overseas extension program teaching a fully accredited course of instruction in the German language.

First Karl would give us a lecture, followed by discussions on some aspect of German or European culture. Then came University of Maryland sponsored field trips to some European city where we would visit and discuss historically significant parts of the city; make trips to art galleries, museums, cathedrals; and have discussions on European literature, architecture and culture.

Learning the language, seeing the country, and coming into a new independence as a person all combined to make the experience of three years living in Germany one I wouldn't have missed for anything. But more than that, I was becoming confident and complete in myself. Along with this newly-discovered life came a realization of how much more there was to learn, and that along with my newly-discovered privileges came new responsibilities.

While flying back home to the United States in March of 1958, with our little Charlie and her new baby brother, Jerry Charles, I wasn't even remotely afraid that the pilots didn't know what they were doing. It was as if the new grown-up security and maturity in me was something I could trust to be present in other people too. That was a tremendous relief!

7

Darkness and Light

The Fort Benning that had stretched out its welcoming arms to a greenhorn officer candidate years before now received an experienced first lieutenant, who was more than ready to attend the Infantry Officers' Advanced Course.

Adjusting to living back in the United States after three glorious years in Germany was not easy. The pace of life in America seemed so rapid and hectic after the leisurely days I had spent with other military wives dawdling over long lunches at sidewalk cafes or strolling through the narrow cobblestone streets and shopping areas of the many interesting European cities.

I had first visited Benning as a new bride. Now, I was returning five years later as a world traveller and mother with two children. How different things seemed.

One habit that wasn't easy to break was having servants to help run the house. But I finally did make peace with the idea. And so even though we couldn't really afford it, we hired a maid and housekeeper as did some of the other military wives.

Nine months later, Jerry completed his infantry instruction and was posted to Fort Devens, Massachusetts. But we circuitously got there by way of a six-week stay at Camp Wolters, which was located in Mineral Wells, Texas. There, Jerry learned to fly helicopters.

He took to helicopters like a child takes to ice cream. Soon he had "soloed" and was talking as though he had been flying helicopters all his life. He would continue to fly them, on and off, for the rest of his military career.

Fort Devens was located in what seemed to me a beautiful, New England paradise. How wonderful it was late in the year when approaching fall reached out its fingers and turned each tree leaf to gold, red, brown or yellow.

And the silver birch! They joyously leaned across the narrow county roads straining to touch the hands of the trees that grew on the other side of the lanes. On weekends we couldn't resist packing the children in the car and driving for hours, captured by the wonder of God's creation.

At Devens we were on a "temporarily permanent" basis once again, settling down for two years this time, two years packed with joy—and tragedy.

Tragedy came first. In the midst of a winter so severe the snow reached to the eaves of the houses, I found myself pregnant again. It was too soon, I thought, after the birth of our son Jerry, who was daily engaged in giving new meaning to the phrase "the terrible twos."

Little hyperactive "Butch," as we called him, was into more mischief than I could get him out of. So instead of welcoming the thought of another new little life to love and cuddle, I resented the child growing in my womb. At Fort Devens, I could not find affordable household help as I had at Fort Benning. I was on my own.

One day I was sweeping gritty crumbs from the kitchen floor where Butch and his sister, Charlie, had just upended a box of cornflakes. The sparkle in their eyes proved to me that it hadn't been an accident. I was exasperated with them, and my stomach hurt.

Feeling sorry for myself with all the work I already had to do and not looking forward to having another infant in diapers, I exploded, "How can I stand to have another child when I can hardly take care of the two I have!"

I was to deeply regret those words, one May morning when second son Gregory Jerome made his entrance into the world. Jerry came to visit me in the hospital and was sitting beside my bed. He was bright and cheerful as usual.

Then the doctor came in with a drawn look on his face and pulled up a chair. *That was odd*, I thought. He was usually in such a hurry he didn't bother to sit down.

Once again I tried to put to rest the uneasy feeling I'd had ever since I'd realized in the delivery room that my baby hadn't cried and that the doctor hadn't spanked him. But my uneasiness had increased when no one had brought the baby to me so I could look him over for myself.

All the resentment I'd felt at being pregnant had long since vanished and been replaced by an eagerness to cuddle and love our new baby. "The baby's all right, isn't he?" I asked, before the doctor could say anything more than, "How are you feeling this morning?"

"Not exactly," he answered in a hollow, brusque tone that could have been a cover-up for a tender heart. Then he turned and spoke more to Jerry than to me, as if he thought it would be easier talking to Jerry.

"I hate to tell you this, Lieutenant Curry, but your child is afflicted with a malformation technically known as spina bifida. I won't burden you with the technicalities. You can read more about it in the literature I've asked my nurse to prepare for you.

"Basically what it says is that the spine is malformed, and spinal fluid is seeping through an opening at the base of the baby's spine."

"Oh, no!" I moaned. "But surely it can be fixed, surgically, I mean?" I blurted out.

"Sometimes a surgical repair can be effective for a few years," he said guardedly, still talking to Jerry instead of to me. "But we don't advise it in most cases. You see, the condition is usually accompanied by contraindications."

"Contraindications? What kind?" The questions came from Jerry. My tears were streaming too fast for words, unnamed fears clutching at my heart.

There was a long pause as the doctor weighed his words very carefully. Finally he said, "It's up to you," then shrugged his shoulders as if the burden was too great for him too. "In some in cases surgery is successful, in some it isn't. Even where surgery succeeds, the child usually becomes an invalid. I'm afraid that in your case, your son will die before he grows to adulthood."

The doctor rose abruptly and left the room, closing the door behind him. Jerry and I were swallowed up in the agony of a grief we had never known. I fumbled to take hold of his hand, and we prayed that God would guide us in the decision we had to make, to risk the baby's life with surgery before he was strong enough to survive it, or . . .

A few days later, I was released from the hospital, and before the end of the week, a voice on the telephone said the baby was ready for a nursing-home placement. The hospital was not equipped for long-term care for chronic cases.

When we went to the hospital to get little Gregory, one of the nurses tried to be kind: "Don't torture yourself by taking him home, Mrs. Curry. It's better if you don't get too attached to him because . . ."

A lump in her throat kept her from finishing the explanation, but it was unnecessary. The reason I wanted to take him home was that no nursing home would give him the loving care I could, for whatever length of time he had to live. I wanted to do all I could for my baby.

And so life stopped for me as I took care of Gregory around the clock. Every forty-five minutes, I had to change his bandages carefully, because the spinal fluid leaked out on a continuous basis and there was a constant danger of infection.

In less than a month, baby Gregory was so weak he couldn't properly suck from his bottle. The result was that he began a long slide into serious dehydration and developed trouble breathing.

When Jerry and I recognized the seriousness of his condition, one that a mother's love couldn't alleviate, we took him to the hospital for intravenous feeding and went home to our other children to spend the rest of the night in prayer.

"Lord, help him," Jerry cried out pleading with God. "Perform the miracle of healing we know you're capable of. Or take him to be with You in heaven. But have mercy. Don't make him continue to live in this horrible condition, struggling for every breath. We ask it in the name of Jesus, amen."

Well into the night, when we had prayed in every way we could think of, we rose from our knees and fell exhausted into bed.

That night the ceiling of our bedroom seemed strangely illuminated. Even with our eyes closed, we were still aware of a mysterious light. No audible words were spoken to us, but we sensed the presence of the Lord Himself—that He was there, responding to our prayers. We had put Gregory into His hands, and His presence had come to assure us that He would do whatever was best for Gregory and for us.

Comforted, we went to sleep, released from the weariness of heart that for weeks had enveloped us. The next morning, a telephone call from the hospital told us that Gregory Jerome had slipped away during the night, perhaps at the very moment when we saw and felt God's intense presence.

At the simple graveside service, and during the days and weeks that followed, I had a supernatural peace about it all.

Comforting words from the Book of Job were often in my mind. Job 1:21 says that the Lord gives and the Lord takes away, but blessed be the name of the Lord.

I did feel guilty at the time wondering if my resentment during the early part of the pregnancy had anything to do with the imperfection of little Gregory's otherwise perfect body. But I didn't dwell on these guilt feelings, neither would they change what happened nor affect how I felt. Since Jesus had already borne my guilt on the Cross, there was nothing more I needed to do but accept His sacrifice.

Now desperately I wanted to have another child, to fill up the aching emptiness of my heart and arms which had been robbed of their baby. My entire being—emotional, spiritual, psychological, and physical—cried for another child. And just as God promised, the Lord gave me the desire of my heart.

I was pregnant before Jerry left in August for a six-month stint at the University of Nebraska for a "bootstrap program," an accelerated cram course for completing his work toward his bachelor's degree. Now, I regretted that I had no housekeeping help.

Pregnancy and two lively little ones to keep up with all by myself made for a difficult winter in 1960. No wonder my stomach hurt so often. I had to get someone to dig me out of the snow every time I had to go to the commissary for groceries or to the clinic to keep a doctor's appointment.

Since we had moved into base housing just a short time before Jerry left, I hadn't gotten well acquainted with our neighbors, and my familiar enemy—loneliness—moved into my life to add to my other miseries. But I didn't allow myself to complain, even silently. I didn't dare. The experience with Gregory was too fresh in my mind.

Three months after Jerry returned to be with us, on April 14, a beautiful day in early spring, the eagerly-awaited Toni René arrived. From the first, she was an utterly delightful baby with beautiful large brown eyes, a quick smile, curly hair, and a beautiful caramel-tan complexion. Everyone fell in love with her at first sight.

Weeping had endured for a night, but joy did come in the morning, just as the psalmist had said it would. For some days, life seemed more or less a mountaintop experience. But we can't live on the mountain forever.

In a few short weeks, Jerry was gone on maneuvers again, and by the time Toni was eight months old, we were uprooted from quarters and on our way to what I thought was the far end of the world.

Occasionally, during the years of painful comings and goings, Jerry and I would pause and look at one another, remembering the childhood certainty we felt that God had some important plan for our lives together.

"Do you suppose that you might become a general someday?" I'd ask him, amazed at my own audacity to even suggest such an impossible thing.

"If God wills it," Jerry would shrug. And we'd laugh together at the statistical improbability of such a thing and talk about something else.

But even when we didn't talk about it for long months at a time, or about the dream of the chateau with crystal chandeliers that Jerry had shared with me as we had sipped milkshakes at Jimmy's Restaurant years before, we knew that God had a plan for us, as He does for all His children.

We sensed that all we needed to do was to be faithful to look to Him and He would prepare us for it and fit us into it. Perhaps the hardships we had experienced were part of that preparation.

8

East and West

*To every thing there is a season,
and a time to every purpose under heaven.*
—Ecclesiastes 3:1, KJV

Leaving Fort Devens to drive from the east coast to the west, the children and I watched the amber waves of grain and purple mountain majesties through the car windows. Jerry was reassigned to the U.S. Army Language School at Monterey, California to study French and the children and I had time to explore the Monterey Peninsula, the city of Carmel-by-the-Sea and Carmel Valley.

After Jerry graduated, the Army in all of its pernicious wisdom assigned him to Korea. How this was supposed to utilize the foreign language he had mastered was more than I could fathom. Never once during Jerry's more than thirty years of service in the military were we stationed in an area where French was spoken.

My assignment, as soon as he left was to finish getting us settled into a new house. After two weeks of being without Jerry and riding herd on three children—one three months old, one two and a half years old, and one five—I realized that this seemingly manageable task was more than I could safely handle in my weakened physical condition.

Not long after Jerry went to Korea, all the emotional turmoil and loneliness resulted in something far worse than a simple stomachache. I landed in the hospital in the intensive care unit, on the critical list, with a bleeding ulcer.

There I remained for twenty-one days, while the children were farmed out to three different military families I hardly knew. Learning of my need, these families had immediately stepped forward to help in every way possible. Forever, I remain indebted to them.

It was one of the most challenging situations I have ever been through. In similar circumstances I've not hesitated to help out other families in dire need, but it was not easy for me to accept such favors from these wonderful families.

The hospital wasn't my idea of paradise either, though it was a temporary respite from responsibilities that were far more physically and emotionally demanding than I had suspected. I was too sick to write Jerry, and afraid to let anyone call and tell him how ill I was. I didn't want to bother him, especially with the distance between us so great and his not being able to affect the situation.

Evidently the ulcer was an old story, which had begun with that stomach pain that I had experienced in Germany and at Fort Devens. Unfortunately it had never been properly diagnosed, even though I'd had the problem for years. In fact, a doctor at Fort Devens had actually told me that there was nothing wrong with my stomach that a good laxative couldn't cure.

Surgery was advised as soon as I arrived at the hospital, but because Jerry wasn't there to give his consent, and because I was in no condition to speak for myself, other less drastic measures were taken.

How I wished my parents weren't on the other side of the United States and that my husband wasn't halfway around the world! I desperately needed family support.

Gradually, as the weeks went by with the bleeding under control, the pain subsided, and when my strength started returning, I was released from the hospital. Though I was still in a weakened condition, I gathered my children together and tried to regain some sense of family.

Jerry, whose primary duty was being the U.S. Army Advisor to the South Korean Aviation School, lived in the southeastern city of Kwang-Ju, Korea. It was a primitive area without much in the way of infrastructure. For example, a phone call had never before been placed between Kwang-Ju and the United States.

One of Jerry's additional duties was to provide advice and assistance to the area's military and civilian communications systems. When he learned through the Red Cross that I had been hospitalized and was now released, he worked with the local Korean phone company and arranged to make the first overseas phone call from Kwang-Ju to the United States.

It wasn't a good connection, but I could understand his voice and we were able to converse a little, which greatly boosted my morale and my spirits. But it was also frustrating and my attempts to call him back were unsuccessful. The children never did get to hear him which caused much disappointment and unhappiness.

The last straw came one night when I was showing a home movie film Jerry had sent us from Korea. The children were viewing it with me. When Jerry walked across the movie screen, big as life, six-year-old Charlie let out a cry of welcome and ran across the room to hug him.

Instead of encountering the expected warm response of a flesh and blood Daddy, she ran into the hard wall behind the screen from which the picture had been wiped out by her shadow. Crushed with disappointment, and with a bump on her head, she sat down on the floor heartbroken and began to sob.

"I want my Daddy! I want my Daddy!"

Her distress set off a chain reaction. In two minutes, son Butch was crying too, then baby Toni, who was too young to know what it was all about. I turned the projector off, snapped on the lights and vowed not to show any more movies of Daddy.

How it happened I don't know, but the next thing I knew I was sitting on the floor with the children. Toni was in my lap and as I tried to comfort all three of them, dammed-up tears of self-pity streamed down my face and I began to cry.

"I want your Daddy, too," I bawled. The four of us sat there sobbing, a study in hurt, disappointment, frustration, self-pity and grief. My crying was so upsetting to the children that they stopped crying and tried to comfort me.

But after that little episode, something happened inside me. A finality set up in my spirit that required action. Either Jerry would have to be returned to me and the children, or we would have to be sent overseas to join him.

This business of living apart had to end. Had it been a time of war, I could have handled it. But this was peace time, I was not well and my family was in crisis. And we hadn't married to spend our lives apart. I know that many other military wives were in the same predicament as me. How they coped I didn't know, but clearly I wasn't doing well. Performing the duties of both mother and father was draining what little strength I had left in me, and I couldn't afford to hire someone to help me with the children and the housework.

I found myself constantly having to cope with problems that would have been nonexistent if Jerry had been with us. It was too much to bear and I was determined to do something about it. So I took my case to the local military and they tried to intercede for me. Quickly it became evident that having Jerry returned back to the United States was not going to happen, but there was a possibility that we could be sent to join him in Korea.

The blockage was Jerry's headquarters, the United States Military Advisory Group in Korea. The chief personnel officer was philosophically opposed to having American families live in the theater of operations, though a few were already authorized and living there. So he disapproved every one of our requests to be united as a family.

Finally, in desperation and after much futile haggling with him, Jerry appealed his case to the equivalent of the Supreme Court, Major General Sydney C. Wooten, the commanding general. Once personally briefed by Jerry, he proved to be most understanding. Quickly he slashed through the red tape, brushed aside the protests of the colonel in charge of personnel actions and had his headquarters prepare the way for us to join Jerry in Korea, even though this meant transferring Jerry from Kwang-Ju to Pusan, a large port city at the southeast tip of Korea.

Hardly back on my feet from the debilitating hospital stay and with no one to help me, I tackled the most difficult assignment of my life—moving our entire household, myself and our three small children—from the United States to a foreign country.

What frantically busy days they were! Getting passports, visas, and shots for me and the children, putting the house in the hands of a real estate agent to sell, making arrangements to sell the car and sorting out all our belongings into four different shipment groups.

Some things had to travel with us to Korea, some had to be sent along ahead of time so we could set up housekeeping as soon as we arrived, and some things had to be packed for storage in the United States. And there were still other things we would continue to need in our California home until the day of our departure.

Trying to do the mental and physical sorting with little Butch trying to help should have earned me a Medal of Honor. At times it was overpowering, what with baby Toni crying, the dog barking, and the doorbell or phone ringing.

I remember vividly one day when Butch's big brown eyes were so drooping with sleepiness that he could hardly hold them open. For half an hour I sat beside his bed trying to get him to take a nap. But whenever I put him down, he popped right back up again, like a weighted toy programmed to defy me, refusing to give up. Little did I realize at the time that he was a child afflicted with Attention Deficit Disorder.

But I was determined that he wasn't going to get the best of me. He was equally determined that I wasn't going to get the best of him. Having far more energy than I did, he finally won, and I gave up. So nothing could be done but let him out of bed, while I returned to my packing.

Not long after I left him alone, I heard him screaming to be rescued. He had climbed into the clothes dryer in the laundry room and couldn't get out. After I extricated him from that predicament,

I gave him a scolding I hoped he wouldn't soon forget, and again turned my attention to the packing.

Shortly I heard the sound of canned goods thudding onto the kitchen floor. I found him standing on a chair, tossing groceries over his shoulder while delightedly mumbling, "Help Mom clean out the kitchen."

I'm sure he couldn't understand why I paddled his bottom for that though I patiently tried to explain. Sniffing, he headed for the locked screen door, pulling a box of toys along behind him. I heaved a sigh of relief, confident he was going to sit and watch the passing traffic through the screen while he played quietly for a change.

But I sighed too soon. An emergency call from a neighbor half-way down the block said my active little two year old was toddling along in front of her house wearing nothing but a soggy pair of training pants. He had apparently unhooked the screen by pushing up on the hook with a long-handled toy.

In those days hyperactivity in children was recognized by the medical profession, but the only treatment was the doctor's telling the distraught mother not to worry, that the child would eventually outgrow the condition. Though I wanted to believe the doctor, I secretly doubted that I would see Butch outgrow it. He never did.

I could hardly believe it when—in spite of everything, including the sad disappearance of our much-loved terrier, Rex, a few days before—Charlie, Butch, Toni, and I finally boarded a flight for Seoul, Korea on December 22, 1960.

Whether I could believe it or not, we were actually on our way to live with Daddy, who had been transferred to Pusan. It was one of the few locations in Korea where dependents were then permitted to live.

9

A Time of Depression

Have not I commanded thee? Be strong and of a good courage;
be not afraid, neither be thou dismayed: for the
LORD thy God is with thee whithersoever thou goest.
–Joshua 1:9, KJV

How big the Pacific Ocean seemed. I thought the flight in the old "Flying Tiger" C-54 aircraft out of San Francisco would never end. We stopped for refueling in Hawaii, then again at Wake Island. From there we flew to Japan and spent the night.

The next day—or was it the day before? Flying with the sun and crossing the International Date Line had me so confused I hardly knew what year it was. Finally, we landed in Seoul, Korea. I literally fell into Jerry's welcoming arms. What a relief it was to let him take charge of everything. It was a strange new land, but somehow the children and I felt that we had come home.

With the family reunited in time for the Christmas holidays, and with the ready availability of inexpensive, devoted household help once again, my life became easier and more joyful than it had been for a long time. Within three months of arrival, all ulcer-producing anxieties were put to rest.

Evidently I relaxed too completely into Jerry's arms because, soon, another baby was on the way.

We had joined one of seventeen American families living in the Hialea Military Compound in the southern port city of Pusan, behind an eight-foot-high barbed-wire fence. All night long huge security lights illuminated the fence and armed soldiers patrolled the outside of the fence in their machine gun jeeps.

But our home was unbelievably spacious and comfortable, not the very primitive mud hut that I'd been willing to live in just to be with Jerry. Still, there were a few things that fell short of perfection—such as the water supply. The Army had its own filtration system, but still the water was a muddy brown. There was always a dark ring in the bathtub, and in a short time white clothing turned a drab, khaki color.

Even though we shopped exclusively at the post commissary, all our fresh vegetables had to be thoroughly washed in a chlorine water solution before they were safe to eat. When we wanted to eat at a Korean restaurant on the other side of the barbed wire, we were restricted for safety's sake. There were only two restaurants in the city able to pass the Army's rigid health inspection standards.

Shopping for clothing and other bargains in the town was conscience-rending as crowds of children followed us everywhere, their eager hands outstretched for the chocolate or chewing gum that they expected us to give them. It was recommended that we leave our valuables on the base, because the local people were eager to steal from us since we appeared to have so much more than them.

Korea, still recovering from the ravages of war, was quite an experience for an American woman in those days. I arrived gawking at everything I saw, and when we left, I was still gawking.

There was always something unbelievable to see, such as the mentally ill roaming the streets, or children with stomachs distended from hunger and internal infections. Dead bodies lay in the middle of the street because, according to local custom, anyone who touched a dead body or moved it was held responsible for burying it.

My two household servants tried to give me a crash course in understanding the Korean people and their customs. My male house servant was an intelligent, literate young man who had deserted from the North Korean Army. Additionally, I had a "Mama-San" who was in her middle thirties. She was married and had four children.

Because her husband had left her and was not providing any support for the children, I felt sorry for her and kept her in my employ long after I discovered that she was stealing from me.

Aside from the pilfering, "Mama-San" and House Boy Kim were excellent help. They cleaned up after everyone and everything, changing the baby's diapers, doing most of the cooking and all of the cleaning, leaving me with little to do but rest and wait for the birth of our new baby.

Soon I gave birth to a beautiful, perfectly formed little girl in the military hospital in Seoul, Korea's capital city. Jerry named her Natasha. The working habits of the Korean nurses was a real culture shock for me. For example, the nurses would empty a bedpan and then, without washing their hands, put a nipple on a bottle of formula for a newborn baby.

American supervisors tried to maintain high standards of hygiene and cleanliness, but it was difficult, at best. It was not long before I was well enough to be discharged and to return home to Pusan, two hundred miles to the south.

Then I was given another opportunity to marvel at hospital routines. Shortly after the birth of darling Natasha, my ulcer flared up again. I found myself confined to the MASH hospital at Pusan where I had to spend another week under American doctors' and Korean nurses' care.

The doctors and nurses were great, but when they weren't looking, odd things happened. I felt that the sooner I got out, the better were my chances for a complete recovery of my health. In fact, it was a wonder to me that we patients survived at all.

Being with Jerry was the top priority in my life. As long as we were together, it was easy for me to cheerfully overlook the less desirable aspects of living in a third-world country. *After all,* I kept telling myself, *living in Korea gave me a new and better appreciation for the American way of life.*

On the other hand, the Koreans were a warm, hospitable people who went out of their way to be friendly and helpful. Many times we entertained Korean officers and their wives in our home and often they reciprocated by inviting us to theirs.

It didn't take me long to adapt to taking my shoes off every time I entered a Korean home, and the straw tatami and hot waxed-paper floors were easy on the feet. We often ate Korean food and really learned to enjoy it.

One of the joys of living in Pusan was being so close to the beautiful South China Sea and its white sandy beaches. Many days we packed lunches, scooped up the children, piled into a Jeep and drove out to the seashore to spend a day with other American families. There were so few of us that we developed a closeness that I have never experienced anywhere else.

Korea was rapidly recovering from the ravages of war. The Koreans were a hard-working, industrious people who were extremely clever with their hands. It seemed they could fabricate or copy nearly anything, using next to nothing for materials.

I marveled watching the Korean civilian fleet of smoke-belching passenger busses, fabricated by hand from fifty-five gallon drums and propelled by worn-out and discarded—but now painstakingly rebuilt—U.S. military truck engines.

Living in such a small American community in an almost primitive foreign country meant that each family had to do more than its share to help the community maintain some semblance of Stateside life. So when other parents asked me to become a Cub Scout Den Mother, I readily agreed even though our son was much too young to participate in the scouting program.

Then, in mid-1963, Jerry got new orders and we headed back across the Pacific Ocean, this time for the Pacific Northwest. We would be living and Jerry would be working at Fort Lewis, in Washington State.

Not unexpectedly, Jerry was constantly leaving on short notice for some type of assignment out of the area. When he was ordered to Fort Bragg, North Carolina, for temporary duty with Special Forces, we decided it would be a good opportunity for me and the children to visit our families back in McKeesport, Pennsylvania.

One week after our arrival back in McKeesport, my ulcer unexpectedly erupted and I hemorrhaged so severely that I was rushed to the hospital in an ambulance. Riding along, with the sirens screaming, I knew I was critically ill and probably dying. It seemed that I was sliding down a narrow dark tunnel with a tiny pinpoint of light at the far end. And the light was flickering as if to go out. Somehow knew that if it went out, my life on earth was over.

How effortless it is to die, I thought. *And how hard it is to live—far too many rough, deep valleys and too few mountain peaks . . .*

But then the pinpoint of light flickered brighter. Somehow I was glad. I was lying on a hard operating table, drifting in and out of consciousness. The concerned eyes of several doctors and nurses, in their sterile wrinkled green operating room scrubs, peered down at me from over their white surgical masks. Then there was nothing.

Regaining consciousness in the recovery room hours later, I caught bits and snatches of conversation that said a third of my stomach had been removed to rid me of a very large duodenal ulcer which had almost cost me my life.

Because I was so desperately sick and in such excruciating pain during the first few days following the surgery, I suspected that I was dying from cancer and believed that the doctors were trying to shield me from the truth. Fortunately, I was wrong. The doctors were telling me the truth. All I had to do was will and fight to live and get well. But that was easier said than done.

School was about to start and I was laid up in the hospital again with Jerry away at Special Forces. We had to do something with the children and the logical thing seemed to be to enroll them in the local school in Liberty where Jerry's parents lived.

Charlie and Butch were thrilled to leave behind their West Coast schools and to be enrolled in the Pennsylvania school where their father had attended so long ago. The timing for them was providential.

But for me lying in McKeesport Hospital, everything that could have gone wrong went wrong in full measure. Every day of convalescence seemed to have its own unique emergency.

First, a serious malfunction occurred in the machine that was pumping fluid from my stomach. When my mother, who was spending the night beside my bed, noticed that I had suddenly stopped breathing, she ran for help. If it hadn't been for her watchful eye, the outcome might have been quite different.

Next, I developed a severe allergic reaction to the penicillin I was given to ward off infection even though I had taken penicillin many times before and never experienced an allergic reaction. Then I contracted a bad cold, my bed having been placed directly under a drafty window in a too-crowded ward.

Looking back on those distressing days, I'm not surprised that at times I wanted to die. But as the days passed, and the pain diminished, I often thought of the needs of my family. Thinking of Jerry and the children, I struggled to develop a strong will to live.

Within two months, at the end of Jerry's temporary duty assignment at Fort Bragg, I was able to return with him to Fort Lewis and resume my duties there as a wife and mother. For a while things went well. My health, so long sapped by the ulcer, improved dramatically, and I gradually gained new physical strength.

Fort Lewis was a lovely place to rear children. The Pacific Northwest was beautiful and green, with lots of safe wild animals, and the children roamed freely and safely throughout the Fort's housing area. Life seemed almost normal for a change.

There were even relaxed Saturday afternoons when we loaded the children in the car and drove across the mountains to watch my cousin, Bill Robinson, play baseball for the Yakima Braves.

There was nothing to suggest that it was "the calm before the storm." But suddenly this short-lived idyllic time was shattered. In the spring of 1965 a telegram arrived from the Department of the Army which ordered Major Jerry Ralph Curry, Assistant Division Aviation Officer in the G3 Section, to form the 220th Aviation Company—personnel and equipment—and lead it to Vietnam. There it would join other units which were forming up to be among the first U.S. combat troops to enter the Republic of South Vietnam.

The children and I would be alone again. Jerry would be halfway around the world for no telling how long. It wasn't going to be easy. But duty called and the children and I were determined to do our part. Somehow, no matter how difficult it might become, we would make it.

More than that, I was soon to learn that all the hardships we had endured as a family had toughened me considerably. All over the nation women were saying good-bye to their men and sending them off to war. I was only one of many and was confident that God would give me strength and courage.

10

Answered Prayer

This is the confidence we have in approaching God:
that if we ask anything according to his will, he hears us.
And if we know that he hears us—whatever we ask—
we know that we have what we asked of him.
—1 John 5:14–15, NIV

The children and I went down to the 220ᵗʰ Aviation Company area to see Jerry off. He and a couple dozen of his men were loading their gear on large commercial busses for the trip to McChord Air Force Base where they would board a military passenger jet for the flight to Vietnam.

Parting was made easier when at the last moment we were informed that it would not be necessary for us to move out of military quarters while Jerry was fighting the war. A new policy decision that was made that week allowed us to remain in the quarters we'd occupied for the last two years. So many families had recently shipped out of Fort Lewis that too many family quarters were standing empty and the Army was losing too much allowance money from the failure to rent the unoccupied quarters.

In addition to having our friends and the family facilities of Fort Lewis made available to us, there was an added bonus. The children wouldn't have to change schools, teachers and school mates. This was a blessing indeed.

In Vietnam, the specific assignment of Jerry's aviation company was aerial reconnaissance, gathering intelligence about enemy movements and activities from the air, spotting enemy units from the air, radioing for U.S. Marine fighter planes to destroy them, and then marking the targets with rockets. From my perspective, too much of this kind of flying was done at very low altitudes. Several times a day I prayed God's protection over all our men and women serving in Vietnam, especially for Jerry's 220th Aviation Company. My loneliness diminished when I thought of the other families who were going through the same thing.

On one hand my concern and prayers for Jerry's safety delivered me from self-pity and from dwelling too long on my own loneliness and difficulties. On the other hand there was always that thought that one day I might hear that dreaded knock at my door with a strange officer in uniform saying, "Mrs. Curry, I regret to inform you that . . ."

Jerry's unit was now flying daily combat missions and his letters were full of details about those reconnaissance missions. He was flying for the South Vietnamese forces stationed in I Corps, located in northernmost South Vietnam, as well as flying in support of the U.S. Third Marine Division.

The letters made the war vivid to me in a way that the newspapers, TV and radio reports never did. But still I tuned in as often as possible to the seemingly never-ending news on TV, complete with films of battle scenes. After a while, it seemed to me and the children that the whole war was being fought in our backyard!

Kneeling by my bed at night, standing at the sink washing dishes, driving the children down the tree-lined highway in our VW bus—wherever I was, whatever I was doing—I prayed many anxious prayers for Jerry and the 220th.

While I was growing in my confidence that God was answering my prayers, I still had difficulty sleeping some nights. It was one thing to say that I trusted God. It was something else to know the reality of it. Yet I was learning that trust was possible and I was doing better than just surviving.

Still, sometimes I jumped at the sudden ringing of the telephone—afraid someone might be calling to inform me that something had happened to Jerry. And sometimes when I finally drifted off to sleep in the wee hours of the morning, I woke up startled, with an intense feeling that Jerry was in danger.

One night I remember getting out of bed and kneeling on the floor. "Lord," I prayed, with all the fervency in me, "this constant state of fear isn't good for me or the children. Please put Your arms of protection around Jerry and guard him and guide him in all that he does. Put Your protection around him like an impenetrable bulletproof bubble. Don't let any harm come near him. Let there always be a bright, unflickering light at the end of his tunnel. All this I ask in the name of Jesus."

I was more than a little overemotional and a little fearful, but I wanted God to know that I wasn't taking "no" for an answer. I expected Him to answer my prayer.

Then I climbed back into bed. Though the prayer hadn't been very religious-sounding, somehow, supernaturally, I knew that a connection had been made. Something between God and me was finally settled.

From that moment on, my daily prayers took on a renewed confidence that God was hearing me. And for the first time in a long while, I started getting a full night's sleep.

Being rested was important, for I had to be strong, patient and even-tempered to take care of the children—Charlie was 12, Butch was 9, Toni 6, and Tash 4. Each morning, I got them off to grammar or nursery school before going to my job as a volunteer dental assistant at the Fort Lewis Dental Clinic.

I felt I needed a job to help me maintain contact with the adult world, and to keep a scheduled routine in my life. And I was determined never to again fall into a rut of loneliness and self-pity, nor did I want to be sick again.

But in spite of successfully coping with Jerry's absence in every positive and sensible way possible, about a month before he was due to return home from Vietnam, I was so tired and run-down that I had to drag myself off to see a doctor.

He put me through a battery of tests, none of them conclusive, but the results worried him so much that he insisted on immediate hospitalization for further diagnostic evaluation. The results came back quickly and seemed to confirm his tentative diagnosis. He felt that my condition was serious and that I might be suffering from a terminal illness.

Based on the evidence at hand, he couldn't be certain, but that didn't matter. I was so anemic and had lost so much weight that I believed that my condition must be terminal.

I decided not to tell anyone about my poor health until I had an opportunity to welcome Jerry home and spend time with him. So against the doctor's orders, I went ahead with my plans.

The children flew to Pennsylvania to stay with my family while I flew to Hawaii to meet Jerry for a second honeymoon and a week in the sun. After three years of living in Washington State I could use a little sun. Only afterward, I decided, would I break the grim news to him.

I thought our week together would be one last final fling before putting my affairs in order and getting ready to die. From the nature of my symptoms, one of which was an extreme pain in my throat, my self-diagnosis was that I had contracted Hodgkin's disease, and that it was so far advanced that it was incurable. Jerry's sister had died of it and I remembered both her symptoms and her horrible suffering during the last days of her life.

But though my intentions were the best, meeting Jerry in Hawaii was disastrous. Try as I might, I was unable to hide my pain from his observant eyes, and after only two days together, I didn't have enough energy to crawl out of bed one morning.

There was nothing left to do but confess to him how ill I was. Immediately he took me to the local military hospital. There the examining physician gave me medication to control the pain and recommended that we return to the mainland on the next flight out.

Back at Fort Lewis, another series of tests at the hospital determined that I didn't have a terminal illness after all, just a painful, weakened condition resulting from a combination of dangerously acute anemia—I always found it impossible to eat properly when

Jerry was gone—and thyroiditis, both of which started responding favorably to treatment.

Jerry's new assignment was to attend the U.S. Army Command and General Staff College at Fort Leavenworth, Kansas. So we closed out our quarters at Fort Lewis and drove back across our wonderful country to McKeesport, where we were reunited with the children and our parents.

It was a leisurely drive, one during which we took in every tourist attraction and trap along the way. Slowly I started getting back on my feet again. It looked like I was going to live after all.

And every time I looked at Jerry, I had wonderful evidence that the Lord had heard and answered my prayers for him. He had come through that year of combat totally unscathed. Furthermore, although many of his men had been wounded, none of their wounds had been fatal. Every man in his company came back alive.

The whole experience brought sharply to focus the power of prayer. *Perhaps I should have prayed more for myself?*

Students at the Command and General Staff College were highly competitive. From day one they were told how important it was to stand high in the class at graduation. Future assignments and opportunities to attend the War College would be partially based on class standing.

But Jerry saw it differently. He felt that he had willingly sacrificed his family and had given the Army his best during the year he had spent in Vietnam. He was determined that his family would come first this year and that he would devote quality time to us.

We were thankful and appreciative that he was putting us first. I was especially thankful since I still had a long way to go with my recovery. And his decision was a blessing in another way. Our son, Jerry Charles, was having a very difficult time academically and there was no way I could have handled the situation alone.

It was a joy and comfort to be able to turn our son and his problems over to my husband. Each night they sat at our kitchen table going over young Jerry's homework. At the end of the school year we decided to hold him back a grade, much to the consternation of his teacher.

But in the long run it turned out to be the right thing to do. The next year he got his feet on the ground academically. And while he never became a gifted student, he was able to keep up with his peers and later go on to graduate from college.

The year ended on a high note when once again we found ourselves reassigned back to Germany. All the painful lessons I had learned about prayer were about to be reinforced across another ocean.

11

Dear Daddy

But no man can tame the tongue. It is a restless evil, full of deadly poison. With the tongue we praise our Lord and Father, and with it we curse men, who have been made in God's likeness. Out of the same mouth come praise and cursing. My brothers, this should not be.
—James 3:8–10, NIV

In the early summer of 1967, we said good-bye to the many military friends we had made at Fort Leavenworth and drove east. This time we were headed for Heidelberg, Germany, where Jerry was to become part of the Office of the Deputy Chief of Staff for Operations, Headquarters U.S. Army, Europe.

By now we had lived overseas so much of our lives that Mom and Dad and my brothers and sister had come to accept it as a normal part of our lives. So this time it was much easier to leave our parents when the visit to McKeesport was over.

The first eleven months in Heidelberg we lived in an attic on the fifth floor of an apartment building—with no elevator. That meant carrying groceries up ten flights of stairs and carrying dirty laundry down to the washer and dryer located in the basement.

All that, and the matter of supervising children outdoors at play five floors below my kitchen window, gave my legs and lungs more exercise than I thought they needed. Although my body seemed to be holding up, I must confess my disposition suffered a bit.

I still thought housework had to be done to perfection with everything able to pass a white glove test at all times. One day after I particularly wearied myself with going up and down the stairs carrying laundry, I found myself unconsciously cleaning an already spotless kitchen. Thoroughly disgusted at some barely noticeable grease spatters on the tile behind the stove I picked up a dishcloth, wet it with detergent and fumed out loud, "That damned wall!" Then I gave the wall a stare that could have killed an elephant at a hundred yards. And I shouted, "No matter how hard I try, I can't ever keep it clean!"

The words were no sooner out of my mouth than a square of the tile fell out from the wall and crashed onto the top of the stove, chipping the porcelain and cracking the tile squarely in two.

Fearfully the children came racing into the kitchen startled by the crashing explosion. They found me gaping open-mouthed at the new hole in the wall. Then they looked down at the broken tile on the stove top.

It was as if by my words, I had caused the tile to fall, though clearly I hadn't. Painfully, I remembered the guilt I felt when Gregory Jerome was born deformed after one of my verbal outbursts.

"The tongue can no man tame," I rehearsed from one of my Bible readings, and it certainly seemed true this time. I asked God to forgive me, and I resolved to bridle my tongue in the future.

While living in the attic in Heidelberg, Jerry learned an important lesson that I believe saved his life. In the Prague spring of 1968, the Soviet Union and its allies invaded Czechoslovakia.

Since Jerry was in Operations and War Planning, he and his fellow officers worked around the clock. The fear was that this was only a prelude to a general invasion of Western Europe by the Soviets. Such an invasion would probably force NATO to resort to the use of nuclear weapons.

People in Jerry's office seldom slept other than catching a few minutes rest on a metal cot in the basement of the war room. For days at a time they didn't even come home for meals. After a few weeks of this nonstop work, some of the older colonels had heart attacks. All of the officers were worn out.

One day Jerry's youngest brother, David, unexpectedly paid us a visit. He was a paramedic assigned to a field hospital west of Heidelberg.

Shortly after his arrival, Jerry dragged through the door looking as though he was about to collapse.

"What's your middle name?" David shouted at him.

Jerry rubbed his forehead, tightly closed his eyes several times and after about thirty seconds mumbled, "Ralph."

Again David demanded, "What day of the week is it? Not the calendar date, the name of the day?"

Try as he may, Jerry could not name the day of the week.

"Look, brother," David said. "You're about to have a breakdown of some type. If you lose your health, you've lost everything. If I were you, I'd pick up that phone, call back to the Operations Center, and tell them that you're deathly ill and can't come back to work today."

Without hesitation Jerry did just that. I was proud of him. But I was more appreciative of David. And since that day, Jerry has always put his health first. Anytime he's been overworked, which has happened many times through the years, he's always remembered David's admonition. Together, we've found a way to get Jerry away from it all long enough for him to regain his strength and clarity of mind.

Jerry had been promised command of a battalion when we left Fort Leavenworth. Without such an assignment, it would be nearly impossible for him to be promoted. In fact, at that time it was difficult for anyone to exchange lieutenant colonel's leaves for the silver eagles of a full colonel. An infantryman, like Jerry, needed to have a battalion command assignment on his record to be selected.

Because they were determined to take care of their own friends, the personnel officers at European Headquarters did all in their power to prevent Jerry from getting a command assignment. First, there was the question of race. None of the infantry battalions in Germany were commanded by black officers. Then it was a question of the "good old boy" network. If Jerry were given a command assignment, one of the good old boys wouldn't get one.

But God in all His wisdom made it possible for him to be sent back to the Pentagon on temporary duty. And before returning to Europe, he visited the Department of the Army Personnel Office in Washington. They were very forthright with him and promised to support his getting a command, provided he could get some division commander in Germany to request him.

It took a lot of doing, and the calling in of a lot of favors, but eventually Jerry was successful. This was in spite of the obstructions thrown across his path by the "good old boy" personnel officers in U.S. Army Europe Headquarters in Heidelberg.

And to our surprise, the battalion he was assigned to command, Second Battalion, 30th Infantry, was located in Schweinfurt, the city where we had spent three years on our previous tour of duty in Germany.

So we moved from Heidelberg back to our beloved Schweinfurt for the last half of this three-year tour. Jerry, recently promoted from Major to Lieutenant Colonel, looked every bit the warrior he was when the battalion colors were thrust into his strong hands.

For the first time, I became First Lady of a battalion, with all the problems, difficulties, and leadership challenges that come with such a position. In the role of "mother-confessor" to many army wives, some older than I, I was expected to help with the parent-teacher association and various community boards and activities, plus see that the nursery was properly run, that the young people were adequately taken care of, and that the boy and girl scouting activities were properly provided for and supervised by volunteers.

In addition, I was expected to make personal appearances at the drop of a hat, give talks, represent my husband at community functions when he was unable to be present, work to build harmonious relations with the German community, put in appearances at German social affairs, and meet the myriad other demands the Army routinely placed on the wives of battalion commanders back then.

Even though I had earlier been First Lady on a smaller scale when Jerry had commanded a rifle company in Schweinfurt, that was only a prelude to the demands that came with being a battalion commander's wife.

From the beginning, although the challenges made everything else I'd done seem insignificant in comparison, I found the job enjoyable. I also discovered to my delight that my past experiences and the training I'd received from senior army wives had more than groomed me for the job. But I never forgot that it was my husband who wore the rank of the military commission and not me. I was his helpmate, not his co-commander.

The proper role of the spouse of a public official has been perfectly defined by Dennis Thatcher, the husband of Margaret Thatcher, the former prime minister of Great Britain. Though a highly respected and successful businessman in his own right, he thought it not improper to be respectful of his wife's position.

He was never observed challenging her dominant leadership role privately or publicly, nor did he assume to speak for her or her policies to either the news media or the government. He never forgot his public place. He always remembered that it was his spouse who was elected to lead the nation and not him.

In the future when the people of the United States of America elect a woman President—and it may happen in my lifetime—her spouse, well-qualified though he may be, shouldn't muck around in running the federal government.

Jerry was busier than ever. While we were still in Heidelberg, he had begun work on a master's degree in international relations through Boston University's overseas campus program.

Twice a week, after commanding his battalion all day, he jumped in the car and drove two and a half hours to Heidelberg, where he attended classes for three hours, and then drove back home. He would arrive home in the wee hours of the morning, sleep for a little while, grab a quick breakfast and then head back to the battalion to put in another full day.

There were other crucial challenges he had to face during this period. Reflecting the signs of the times, racial unrest broke out in U.S. Army Europe. Many times Jerry had to wade into the middle of unruly mobs and demonstrators and, with the other battalion commanders, try to calm them. It was the battalion commanders' job to see that government and individual property was protected, and that all of our lives were secure.

Like all battalion commanders in Schweinfurt, sometimes Jerry had to sit for hours counseling disgruntled, militant soldiers far into the night. Then he'd come home to steel himself and get ready to meet the harrowing demands of the next day. But instead of tiring him, the challenges seemed to cause him to grow stronger.

During lulls in action, we still managed to work in time for a little travelling and vacationing. Perhaps the most fun we had was skiing. Jerry insisted that we all learn to ski. Since Europe has great skiing, it was a family opportunity we were determined to maximize. So off to the slopes we drove where Jerry got us all up onto skis. While we didn't get any offers from the US Olympic Ski Team, we did have a great time.

I didn't suspect that back in the States trouble was brewing. The first indication of it came in the form of a late night overseas phone call from my mother. "Dad's in the hospital," she explained when I was awake enough to understand.

"He was hospitalized four days ago when he suddenly became deathly ill. The problem is defying diagnosis. X-rays haven't helped the doctors very much. Each day his condition worsens."

The strong concern and worry evident in her voice quickened my spirits and brought me fully awake.

"The doctors did an exploratory abdominal operation today," she continued. "They discovered that a section of the small intestine was adhering to the wall of his abdominal cavity, affecting the heart as well as other vital organs. Gangrene has set in and many hours of surgery were required before he could be sent to the recovery room, and then on to the Intensive Care Unit. In spite of heroic efforts on the part of the doctors, his heart kept stopping and they had to keep shocking it back into action . . . It's been touch and go."

Finally her voice broke, "Charlene, if you want to see your father alive, you'd better hurry."

Jerry's duties made it impossible for him to go with me, so entrusting the children to the care of him and our good friends,

I caught the first plane out, with my tears and prayers unceasing through that long flight.

My fervent hope against hope, while flying home from Germany to Pennsylvania that March of 1970, was that God would get me there in time to see my father before he died.

I wanted to ask Dad's forgiveness for all the times I'd thought he was too strict a disciplinarian when I was growing up. I wanted to thank him for ruling me with an iron hand when my willfulness and innocence would have made me fair game and prey for a wicked world. I wanted to let him know how much I appreciated all the sacrifices he had made for me. I yearned to tell him all those things before it was too late.

I mused on how fast life had moved, on how much my daily responsibilities had crowded out important essentials or caused me to put them off year after year. How long it had been since I'd seen any of my family in the United States!

My brother George met me at the Pittsburgh Airport and drove me straight to the McKeesport Hospital. "How is he?" I asked, my eyes brimming with tears and my throat aching. George only set his lips in a tight line and shook his head.

For days Mom and I sat quietly beside Dad's bed. Then one day after being close to death for so many days and nights, Charley Cooper blinked open his eyes. His gaze traveled slowly around the room noticing the surroundings he'd been too sick to see previously.

"Where am I? And where have I been?" he painfully asked.

"Oh, Dad! You've been here in intensive care—almost dead for days," I blurted out, squeezing his hand. From the light in his eyes and the half smile on his lips, I was certain that he was going to recover. And George and Mom knew it, too.

"Well, I guess I'm alive now!" he said smiling. "Isn't it time to eat?"

His asking for food was a sure sign that the crisis was past. Within a few days, he was released from the hospital and I flew back to Germany, Jerry, and the children.

Seeing my father so near death stirred fresh memories of my own critical illnesses and set me searching to know more of what the true meaning of death-and-life was all about. My search was not from any desire to die, but a wish to better know Jesus, the One who has overcome the last enemy we humans have to face.

In a few months, the racial unrest in Schweinfurt was brought under control and peace and tranquility reigned again in U.S. Army, Europe, but not in our family. About this time military orders arrived reassigning Jerry back to Vietnam for a second tour of duty. This time, instead of flying airplanes, he would be living and fighting in the jungle as the Senior Advisor to a South Vietnamese Infantry Regiment.

So in June 1970, Jerry, the children and I once again left Germany for the United States—and a major turning point in our lives. While Jerry would be fighting once more in Vietnam, the children and I would spend the year in Colorado Springs, Colorado.

12

Turning Point

But you will receive power when the Holy Spirit comes on you.
–Acts 1:8, NIV
Be filled with the Spirit; Speaking to yourselves in
psalms and hymns and spiritual songs, singing and making
melody in your heart to the Lord . . . Jesus Christ.
–Ephesians 5:18–20, KJV

For me and the children ocean crossings had become rather routine. On the east coast of the good old USA, we picked up our two cars and drove to McKeesport. The grandparents were eager to see for themselves how much the children had grown. And we were equally eager to see them and to share the experiences of our just-completed three years in Europe.

None of us foresaw that this joyfully anticipated visit was to be a spiritual turning point of great significance which would catapult us up onto a new plateau of experiential living that we didn't know existed.

To the casual observer it probably looked as if no turning point was needed. Our children were happy, healthy, and well-adjusted. Jerry was clearly super-successful in his career, moving up the ladder with promotion after promotion, as soon as he was qualified. And he was making continual progress in his academic work, too, having just earned an MA in International Relations from Boston University's Heidelberg campus.

Outwardly I appeared to be in good health for a change and was regarded by most as a successful mother and wife, a person who had fulfilled her military First Lady assignments creditably and with style.

That I had survived moving our household fifteen times so far, from one continent to another and then to another—without falling apart—was a major accomplishment. Our marriage was still in good shape, having weathered successfully the various crises that had inevitably come to it, as they do to all marriages—military and civilian.

True, Jerry was scheduled for another year of fighting in the jungles of South Vietnam, never something anticipated with joy by me and the children. But the children were older now, my ulcer was gone, and I was more experienced in coping with the single parent syndrome than I had ever been before.

But if I had stopped to look within, I would have readily admitted that I was far from satisfied with my life. My own near-death from the bleeding ulcer, and my father's close call with his emergency surgery, lurked in the back of my mind.

Such memories kept my inner restlessness stirring, a growing awareness that there just had to be more in life—in God—than I had so far experienced.

As is often the case, my almost invisible inner turmoil and discontent had little to do with the outward circumstances of life. Somehow the whole point of living was escaping me, passing me by. Being a successful mother, wife, housekeeper, and military First Lady wasn't enough. Though I had accomplished much, the sum total of my life didn't seem to add up to being one whole person.

It was impossible for me to put it into words, but there was a dim, growing awareness that something was missing, a vital something that had to be supplied if I was to become the person I was meant to be—the person I wanted to be.

I didn't have any idea what "it" was, but I intuitively knew that if I didn't find out soon, one day I'd be unable to carry on, to finish my course with vigor and purpose, to continue to meet all challenges, to overcome all of life's obstacles.

God was there. But except for dire emergencies, He seemed to be far away. I wasn't as close to Him as I wanted to be. If I did not become more secure in my relationship with Him, I feared the light I had seen at the end of the tunnel, when I was dying, might one day be snuffed out.

Since God had used Mom Curry to meet an earlier spiritual need in my life, before I had gone to Germany as a young bride, it was natural that He would use her again in a more powerful way.

During our stay in McKeesport, Toni, aged ten, and Natasha, aged eight, were baptized at Bethlehem Baptist Church. The baptismal service triggered memories of my own baptism in that church when I was twelve years old. How clean I had felt when I emerged from the water of the baptistery, recessed into the floor beneath a fresco of the Jordan River.

Symbolically I knew that back then the old Charlene had been buried with Christ in baptism and had come up out of the water a new Charlene, raised with Jesus from the dead. It reminded me of the nation of Israel's symbolic baptism when they had gone down into the Red Sea. It had been a wonderful experience for me, just as the sparkle in Toni's and Tasha's eyes told me that it was a wonderful experience for them, too.

Thinking back, I knew I had lost that feeling of closeness to God that I had felt on the day of my baptism. It hadn't lasted long. Except for the often fearful reliance on God in emergency situations, I wasn't living the kind of life God wanted me to have. As I looked back, I realize that over the years I had often been grimly hanging on only by my fingernails.

After the girls' baptism, we all went to Mom Curry's house. Sometime during the evening, Jerry, Toni and I found ourselves seated in Mom's small, neat living room along with Jack Kennedy, a Presbyterian minister, and his wife, Sally, both of whom had just returned from the mission field in Africa. We talked of many things that night, though nothing of great significance. We just shared experiences.

But suddenly the air was charged with an electrical current. Mom Curry was sitting up very straight in her chair, looking intently at Jerry, almost as if she was making a formal speech to an audience of one. I found myself leaning forward to catch every word.

She began with what amounted to an historical review of Jerry's life, remembering aloud how he had always been a good boy, an Eagle Scout with exemplary trustworthiness, not giving her any real trouble in his childhood, serving God in his church, sending his tithes back to the McKeesport congregation even after he left home for military life.

She acknowledged that he had worked hard, had successfully met all the challenges set before him, had earned many well-deserved awards and commendations and had every reason to take pride in his many accomplishments.

I nodded at every complimentary thing she said knowing it all to be true. Toni, who was ten, was perched on a footstool, enjoying being an audience to the grown-up conversation. She nodded her head enthusiastically at every good thing Grandma Curry said.

"Whenever you come to visit," she continued, "mothers in the church hold up their children shoulder-high to let them get a good look at you. They say things like, 'Take a good look at Jerry Curry, because he's a fine man, and I want you to grow up to be just like him.'"

In McKeesport, Jerry had always been admired by grown-ups and children alike. There was something about him that made people almost idolize him, just as I had when we were growing up together.

So it was a surprise when Mom suddenly asked this handsome, well-educated, successful, mature military officer son of hers, "How would you like to become the kind of Christian you think you are?"

My mouth dropped open. Jerry, who had probably been ready to make a modest, "Oh, shucks, mom, it hasn't been so much," reply of some kind, looked shocked. Toni was staring at her grandmother like she had just committed high treason.

While we waited for Jerry's answer, my mind applied the question to the deep-seated need in my own life: *Charlene, how would you like to be the kind of Christian you've been striving to be, with such mixed results—up on the mountain-top one day and low down in the valley the next?*

"Do you mean there's a way to do that?" I interrupted. "A way to be the kind of Christian I want to be . . . all the time?"

Mom nodded then opened her Bible and had us look at some scriptures, scriptures whose meaning until them had been hidden from my understanding. That night they became awesomely clear and plain.

She read aloud, from her well-worn Bible with the limp black leather cover. Some of the pages showed crinkly water spots where tears had wet the pages along with prayers from her heart. The Scriptures I remember best from that evening were the words spoken by John the Baptist, telling the multitudes coming to him for baptism for remission of sins that there was *One* coming after him whose sandals he wasn't worthy to carry. That One, he said, would be the Messiah, the One who would baptize with the Holy Spirit and with fire.

Just as every believer should be baptized with water following the scriptural pattern," Mom explained further, "so should we all be baptized with the Holy Spirit, like John the Baptist said."

She continued, "Jerry, you're about to leave for a second tour in Vietnam, and only heaven knows what awaits you there." She paused. "Son, you need the Messiah's baptism, the one with the Holy Spirit and fire."

To me this sounded strange yet somehow it made sense. But how could someone be baptized with the Holy Spirit? Even though my rational mind questioned it, a solid acceptance was beginning to form. Subconsciously something within me was beginning to believe all that Mom Curry was saying, and eagerness to embrace it was building inside me.

Mom reminded us that Jesus had charged His disciples to wait in Jerusalem for the "promise of the Father." Next she read Acts 1:8 in which Jesus said that after the Holy Ghost—who is the promise of the Father—had come upon them, they would receive power.

That was it! Instinctively I understood that *power* was what was missing in my own life, the power to live life the way I desperately needed to, a way that would please God.

In the early days of the church, the service of "confirmation" confirmed that you had accepted Jesus Christ as the Son of God and Savior and had been baptized with the Holy Spirit. When a Peter, Paul or John placed their hands upon a new Christian's head, miraculous things happened.

For example, in Acts it says: "When Paul placed his hands on them, the Holy Spirit came on them, and they spoke in tongues and prophesied" (Acts 19:6, NIV). That was powerful stuff.

In the same Scriptures, Jesus went on to say that those upon whom the Holy Spirit came would be His witnesses. Intuitively I understood that this was the same experience had by Mary the mother of Jesus and the 120 disciples who at Pentecost were following Jesus' instructions to wait at Jerusalem for the promised Holy Spirit.

Mom continued, "In Luke 11:13, Jesus said that, 'If you, then, being evil, know how to give good gifts unto your children, how much more shall your heavenly Father give the Holy Spirit to them that ask him!'"

Now it was all so plain. I was baffled to think that I'd never noticed these words before, or if I had, I hadn't understood them. I was further amazed that I'd never heard in a church or military chapel that the power of the Holy Spirit was something I could have, simply by asking God for it.

I slid to my knees in front of the couch ready to ask and receive. But by the furrows in Jerry's brow I could see that his analytical mind wasn't convinced.

Now I remember only snatches of the conversation but it concluded with Jerry saying he'd need to give it further study . . . that he wasn't sure an army officer could use such an experience.

Mom Curry stood up and said, "You've become far too sophisticated and educated for me. I don't have enough vocabulary to explain these things to your satisfaction. I just can't get through all those barriers between us since you've become such a learned individual.

"But I know God's Word is true." And then sounding more military than motherly she concluded, "If what I've read to you tonight from God's Word hasn't convinced you, then look at my life. In thirty-eight years, what kind of life have I lived before you?"

"Mom, you've always lived an exemplary life," Jerry said.

"Have I ever lied to you?"

"No, you never have."

"Have I ever led you astray—or recommended something that was not in your best interest? Have I ever given you bad advice or guidance?"

"No, never."

"Well, then, if you can't accept that this work of the Holy Spirit is for you on the basis of what I've read to you from God's Word, then accept it on the basis of the Christian life I've lived before you.

"I received the Holy Spirit back in 1946," she continued, "and it is what has made all the difference in my life. It will make that kind of difference in your life, too."

When she said that I knew she had nailed Jerry because he had the highest regard for his mother. She had "laid a heavy word on him," as they say, one against which I knew he would not fight.

So I wasn't surprised when he quietly said, "Okay, Mom, you win. Let's pray," then he slipped to his knees beside me in front of the red pile couch with Scripture verses hanging on the paneled wall behind it.

Soon I felt Mom Curry's and Jack Kennedy's hands resting on my head, and heard their prayers.

My own prayer was simple and uncomplicated, I can remember it still: "Father God, please give me your Holy Spirit just as You said You would, so I can live the kind of life I should, and so that I can be your witness." That was all there was to it.

They were simple words, from the depths of an uncomplicated heart. But oh, what a profound difference they made in my life!

While I was still speaking, I felt a peace come over me unlike anything I had ever before experienced. It seemed to flow down from the top of my head to the tips of my toes, filling every empty corner of me—every single cell. And not just filling, but overflowing with an awareness that God was in me, somehow completing me. And with His presence, there was such overwhelming joy! I wanted to dance, to sing, to laugh, to cry—and I guess I did all those things at once. I was suddenly whole, complete, for the first time ever, every cell of me bursting with life! I was praising the Lord, thanking Jesus, bubbling over with the love I felt for my God and had never before adequately expressed. The deep feelings that had been dammed up inside me, frustrated by a lack of words, were flowing freely, quenching my thirst to tell Him of my love. What satisfaction, what peace, then came—perfect acceptance by a perfect Lord.

My mind grasped for comparisons. It was a oneness with God surpassing the perfect oneness I had felt with Jerry when we used to dance together in our living room. I'd been utterly abandoned to his leading, and now I felt an even greater harmony with God, my spirit moving along with His Spirit in perfect unison.

I thought of the song my Father used to sing—the song that was his mother's favorite:

In The Garden

I come to the garden alone,
While the dew is still on the roses;
And the voice I hear, falling on my ear,
The Son of God discloses.

And He walks with me, and He talks with me,
And He tells me I am His own,
And the joy we share as we tarry there,
None other has ever known.

He speaks, and the sound of His voice
Is so sweet the birds hush their singing,
And the melody that He gave to me,
Within my heart is ringing.

And He walks with me, and He talks with me,
And He tells me I am His own,
And the joy we share as we tarry there,
None other has ever known.

Even after I went to bed that night, I could still sense the Holy Spirit's presence washing over me. When I awoke the next morning, I felt like a brand-new person. All the old striving in me had vanished—at least for the time being.

The words of King David the psalmist, "I have run through a troop: by my God have I leaped over a wall" (2 Samuel 22:30, KJV), echoed the excitement bubbling up within my spirit. The Lord knew I would need every ounce of it in the days and years to come, as would Jerry!

1947 | *Charlene's parents, Charles & Mamie Cooper*

1950 | *Charlene & Jerry–High School Prom*

1953 | *Charlene & Jerry–High School Days*

1953 | *Charlene, shortly after she married Jerry*

1966 | *Charlene & Daughter Natasha in a Fashion Show at the Officer's Club at Fort Lewis WA*

This is the window from which I watched Jerry jump from the aircraft.

1972 | *Converted WWII barracks where Charlene watched out the kitchen window as Jerry's paratrooper unit jumped from airplanes in the distance*

1972 | *The Curry family at the Hall of Heroes in the Pentagon*

1972 | *The Curry Family at the U.S. Army Command and General Staff College at Fort Leavenworth, Kansas*

1977 | *Charlene & Jerry share a light-hearted moment together*

1981 | *Charlene greeting Lieutenant General Galteri of Argentina.*

1982 | *Charlene & Jerry's mother, Rev. Mercer Curry, visit with Nancy Reagan*

1982 | *Charlene & her special dinner partner–Clint Eastwood*

1983 | *Charlene & Jerry wait for a show*

1984 | *Charlene visits with Barbara Bush*

1984 | *Jerry and Nancy Reagan*

1985 | *On vacation in Austria*

1987 | *Charlene and her mother, Mamie Cooper*

2003 | *Children, grandchildren, spouses, and extended family at Jerry and Charlene's 50th Wedding Anniversary–photo taken by Henry Schulz*

2004 | *Charlene and Jerry's home, "Chateau Antioch"*

2005 | *Charlene and Jerry–Still in Love*

13

Time for Change

Trust in the LORD with all thine heart; and lean not unto thine own understanding. In all thy ways acknowledge him, and he shall direct thy paths. Be not wise in thine own eyes: fear the LORD, and depart from evil. It shall be health to thy navel, and marrow to thy bones.
—Proverbs 3:5–8, KJV

Two days later we left McKeesport for Colorado Springs. But first we stood with Jerry's mother in the driveway, joining hands in a circle with all the family—his parents and mine, and all our brothers and sisters.

Mom prayed God's protection over us for our journey and afterward said that during her prayer God had given her the assurance that no matter what dangers Jerry faced in the war, he would safely return home from his second tour in Vietnam.

Jerry was grinning as he leaned out the window of our VW bus to call out our last good-byes. "Praise the Lord!" he shouted.

I was crying, the joy of love and the sadness of parting mingled together. But I couldn't help seeing the expression on the face of my sister-in-law, Olga, my brother George's wife. Mixed with her love and concern for us was a look of intense exasperation.

It didn't take a lot of imagination to know what Olga was thinking behind those intense dark eyes and a face that tried to look friendly. I could feel her thinking, "Jerry and Charlene have turned into religious fanatics, just like Mom Curry."

I was too full of enthusiasm to let her hostility turn me off. Instead, I almost had to suppress a giggle, suspecting that her own days of not being a "fanatic" were strictly numbered, along with those of everyone else in the family who wasn't yet totally wrapped up in the love of Jesus. No question about it, the new certainty that I was the temple of the Holy Spirit was the most marvelous thing that had happened to me since my conversion, and I didn't intend to stop praying until every member of our extended families had come into that certainty for themselves.

As we drove west across the country toward Colorado Springs, I prayed for each member of our families by name, that they too might have the blessing of the Holy Spirit. We named all our nieces, nephews, cousins, aunts, and uncles. We prayed for Uncle Luke, Aunt Nellie, Aunt Sadie—and Cousin Billy, then playing baseball with the Pittsburgh Pirates—that he would be a powerful Christian example to his teammates.

We were a big family, so there was a long list of names. I spoke about each to the Lord in my prayers from that day on with eager expectancy, kneeling beside my bed with my eyes closed, driving down the highway with my eyes open, as I went about my housework, or drove to the grocery store.

Sometimes it was a conscious, out loud prayer. Other times it was a subconscious, softly spoken inner murmur of thanksgiving, thanksgiving that God was hearing and answering. How different it was now from the anxieties that I had had previously, when I only prayed out of intense need or fear.

Although it didn't happen overnight, as I had expected it to, it did begin to happen. Slowly at first, then with the increasing tempo of popcorn placed over a fire, one by one members of our families accepted Christ as their Savior and Lord. They popped up throughout the Curry and Cooper families and it was fascinating and gratifying to be a small part of it.

Before, where Mom Curry and Jerry's brother Bob had been the only Christians experiencing the fullness of the Spirit. Mom Curry had smoldered faithfully but silently for thirty-four years. Now, in less than a years time, there were many more, including all four of our children. The glow was spreading to others! What a year it was! I regretted that Jerry was in Vietnam and couldn't enjoy it with us.

Back in Schweinfurt, Germany when Jerry had asked me where the children and I would like to spend the year while he went on his second Vietnam tour, we had chorused our answer to him, "Colorado Springs near Fort Carson!" We'd never lived there before, but many of our friends had, and we'd heard so many reports of the perfect weather and the wonderful skiing that we wanted to try it for ourselves.

As we approached the city, darkening blue clouds fast became a thunderstorm and lightning flashes dramatically illumined an area of the city called Skyway. Now, for the first time in my life, I was not afraid of an electrical thunder storm. Instead, I saw it as a magnificent demonstration of the power of a God who loved me.

It was as if the storm was his finger pointing and saying, "This is the place I have chosen for you to live while Jerry's away fighting in the war."

Soon our new address was 1005 Sun Drive, Skyway. A few days later, we left the piles of things still spread around the house and the unpacked boxes of belongings stacked in every corner of the house, and once again took Jerry to the airport. Our eyes misted over as we watched his plane disappear out of sight behind the hot build up of cumulus clouds.

For the first time in our lives we went back to a house that wasn't empty just because Daddy was gone to war for a year. We knew he would be back, and meanwhile, the house was filled with the presence of Jesus, our living Lord. The children were as determined as I was to have a good year.

The first three months sped by and only then did it begin to dawn on me that Jerry was gone, and that he would be gone for a long time—nine more months. That sudden realization had such an impact on me that before I could stop what was happening, I found myself getting depressed.

"What am I going to do?" I asked out loud. Then looking up at the lighted ceiling instead of down at the dark tile floor

I concluded with confidence, "Why, I'm going to get along just fine!"

This new victory in my life wasn't nebulous or theoretical. It was real, something I could put my hand on, something I could take hold of by an act of my will and live out during the days and nights as the children and I looked forward together to the day when Jerry would be back with us again.

14

Little Victories

Finally, brethren, whatsoever things are true, whatsoever
things are honest, whatsoever things are just, whatsoever
things are pure, whatsoever things are lovely, whatsoever
things are of good report; if there be any virtue,
and if there be any praise, think on these things.
–Philippians 4:8, KJV

I won't pretend that the months in Colorado Springs were perfect. Sometimes I didn't behave according to the wonderful new knowledge that God had given me; sometimes I forgot that victory was mine only if I reached out and took it. But considering everything, our lives were unbelievably good.

Practicing the presence of the Holy Spirit in my daily life, which I forced myself to do, trusting it would later become a habit, was starting to work. Loneliness had always been my worst enemy when Jerry was gone, probably because he and I were so close in our thoughts that no other person—except the Lord—was a satisfactory substitute.

When I wrote Jerry and sent him letters and pictures of the children and then opened his letters written on the battlefield, I found I was no longer afraid. Instead of being filled with fear, as I had been on his first Vietnam tour, I sensed the hovering of the angel's wings that we used to sing about so long ago in the choir at Bethlehem Baptist Church.

I could shut my eyes and hear Jerry's voice blending with mine. And I could relive the days when he had sung a solo and the choir joined in the swelling chorus of affirmation, "How Great Thou Art!" God had been real to me in those days, real but untouchable. Now God was right beside me. That comforting knowledge made worlds of difference in every aspect of our lives.

One of the areas where I first noticed a change was in my disposition. I'd always had a terrible temper, easily triggered, accompanied by a critical, complaining tongue. The children learned early in life to behave in ways calculated not to bring on my explosion. Often I'd overhear one telling the others, "Better not do that, because Mom will get mad."

It wasn't just their deliberate misbehavior or mischief that would set my pulse racing and blood pressure soaring. A simple, accidentally spilled cup of milk running over on the table and dripping harmlessly onto the easily cleaned kitchen floor had many times set me stomping my foot, clenching my teeth, and maybe even shedding a few tears of frustration as I seethed with rage. But with the new me, the Holy Spirit was in control, taming my tongue.

One Sunday just a few months after I had knelt beside the couch in Mom Curry's living room, a glass bottle of pancake syrup slipped from my hands and crashed onto the hard tile kitchen floor, bombarding me, the cabinets, walls, and everything else in sight with flying shards of glass and gooey spatters of sticky syrup.

"Oh, no!" I groaned softly, momentarily holding my head in my hands and closing my eyes, afraid to look at the mess. Then I heard a cheerfully resigned, "Oh, well," come from my lips as I smiled, knelt to pick up the broken glass and start cleaning up the syrupy mess so we could leave for Sunday school and church.

When I saw the children lined up in shocked silence in the doorway their mouths open, it dawned on me—*I wasn't angry!* Tash put it into words that rang with unbelief and astonishment:

"Mom! You didn't get mad!"

The five of us looked at each other for a few seconds, then burst into laughter all around. Jerry was away at war and an accident had happened, but we weren't sitting on the floor crying about our awful misery—we were laughing! It took several days for our giggles to subside.

Even so, years later, every once in a while one of the children would say, "Remember the day when Mom dropped the pancake syrup on the kitchen floor when we were living in Colorado Springs?" The reminder was always good for a laugh no matter how unlikely the circumstances.

After the broken bottle experience, every time something would happen that would have made the old Charlene angry, the Holy Spirit helped me to say within myself, "Alright, the choice is up to you. You know you don't have to react in the old ways. In Christ you're a brand-new creature. The old Charlene has passed away if you will just let her lie."

Since then I have found that practicing the presence of the Holy Spirit really does work. Others who have lived the same way tell me that they feel as though there is a quiet inner voice whispering, "Don't do it," or, "Don't say that anymore."

But for me the practice of the presence of the Holy Spirit had to be a constant, deliberate choice. God refused to override my free will. The Holy Spirit, unlike the "unholy spirit," refuses to control our personality. God can influence our lives, but only when we freely cooperate with Him.

Through the grace of God, I was able to yield more and more of myself. And eventually, my new self began to become a habit. With the passing away of temper tantrums came the death of the nagging I'd previously thought necessary in order to force my impossible perfectionist standards on everyone. Now that my inner spirit was set free from self-condemnation, external details and appearances didn't seem nearly so important as before.

The Bible teaches us that the fruit of the Holy Spirit is love, joy, peace, patience, kindness, goodness, faithfulness, gentleness and self-control. Slowly I was finding this to be true. Most of us struggle through life on our own power doing things without considering that the God who created us has a better plan.

An awful bondage fell away as I began to realize that my house was not perfect and neither my children nor my wardrobe or I would ever be perfect. They were, nevertheless, quite acceptable, if I would only yield to the gentle nudging of the Holy Spirit.

During that year of separation, my inborn, do-it-myself striving for perfection died hard, but it did die. It had to! I saw clearly that people set on perfection, never achieve it. Perfection is the enemy of progress, or as Jerry says, "The perfect is the enemy of the good."

There was a related change in Jerry, too. I noticed in his letters a new openness to receive suggestions from other people, a new humility that seemed to say, *I want to keep on hearing from God, and I know that He can speak to me through anyone, the newest buck private as well as the highest ranking general. I'm going to look for opportunities for everyone to make a contribution toward our common goals.*

Every once in a while, he'd write home telling how a knotty problem had been solved through an insight that had come through the least likely fellow in his organization. As he shared these things with me, I tried to practice them in my own life, and often heard through the lips of my children helpful suggestions for handling problems in our family life.

All of us were experiencing a new freedom in God that we'd never found in any other way. There was no longer any need for us to think we were solely responsible for how everything turned out. As long as we conscientiously did our best, put everything into God's hands, and sought His guidance, the outcome was up to Him. We didn't have to feel guilty about our failures—failure seemed to be built into the human system—but we knew that the victory was ultimately with those who followed the Lord's in all things.

In the matter of proper discipline and management of the children, where once I had felt helpless, I now had a new inner power that was bringing peace instead of strife.

One day Natasha was playing a game with marbles in the middle of the living room floor. Little Jerry was playing records in the same room, and Tash's moving about with her game accidentally jolted the needle on her brother's record and scratched it.

He didn't ask Tash to move her play area; he just lifted his foot and kicked the marbles, sending them flying. Some rolled under couches and chairs; some sped along the open hallway and bounced down the stairs into the basement.

Tash ran in and told me what he had done. I confronted him: "Pick up the marbles, Jerry," I demanded of him.

I had suspected for a long time that he was developing an attitude that said: "Women don't have any authority." But now, for the first time, it was blatantly out in the open. Looking me straight in the eyes he said defiantly, "I will not pick up those marbles."

He had never done such a thing before, and for a half a second I felt utterly defeated. Then, what I needed to do came to me, and I did it calmly, quietly, and lovingly, but with Holy Spirit authority.

"In the name of Jesus, pick up every one of those marbles," I commanded.

His defiant spirit wilted. Quickly he picked up every marble, searching each one out until he had found them all.

That day, I recognized that it wasn't young Jerry who had been trying me, but the rebellious spirit within him, a spirit that had persuaded him that I was to feed him, wash his clothes, and get him to school, but was to exercise no control over his life. Then the spirit of youthful rebellion was just beginning to rear its ugly head.

Today, that rebellious spirit seems to have permeated our society. Loss of respect for legitimate authority and the property of others has become a serious problem. And it isn't just confined to children. It is particularly strong in those of my son's generation who are in their forties.

Some are still struggling to learn proper standards of conduct, and what our society should or should not permit or where they themselves should draw a firm line. This is a deficiency in our national spirit that cries out to be addressed.

Changes in my prayer life were among the most remarkable of all the changes I observed in myself. I knew the Bible said we were to pray without ceasing, but I'd found it impossible to do that. I could pray, all right, when I was driving the car, washing windows, or walking the dog, but when I was involved in something that required my whole concentration—like helping one of the children with homework, or figuring out the proportions in a new recipe—there were gaps in my prayers. Now I discovered that even when my conscious mind was thinking about something else, the spirit deep within me was continuing to pray.

I also found far more satisfaction in my prayers than I had formerly. It wasn't possible to complain or grumble or feel sorry for myself when I was busy praising God. Prayer put a different perspective on everything that happened in my life. Prayer kept the presence of the Lord so real to me that sometimes I expected to open my eyes and see Jesus standing right there in front of me.

Another life-changing effect was the development of a new hunger to read the Word of God. Of course I had read the Bible before, but mainly because I was supposed to do it. Sometimes I got something out the reading, but not always, and not a lot.

Often I had put the Bible down, bored with it, promising I'd come back to it later. But after June 1970, my Bible reading was far from dull. The words seemed to leap out, not as the obscure, hard-to-understand words that men had written down a long time ago, but fresh words—what God was personally saying to me now, today.

According to his letters, Jerry had the same new hunger for reading the Bible. Sometimes, he wrote, circumstances would break in such a way that he could read the Bible for most of the day, and he never tired of reading it. The old, dull words were suffused with new life for both of us now that we knew so intimately the Author of them all.

My conversation began to change, reflecting my inner communion with God and his Word. Where once I had specialized in talking about the state of my health, or lack of it—regaling all who would listen with long tales of my illnesses and emergency situations with the children—now that all seemed unimportant.

I used to spend a lot of time shopping for clothes; now clothes were of diminished importance to me. The Holy Spirit was teaching me that what I was on the inside was more important than what I wore on the outside. I wanted the beauty of a peaceful and quiet spirit far more than I wanted to be a fashion plate.

I was beginning to understand that there was nothing God couldn't do for me—or anyone else—if I just let Him work in my life. Every time I yielded more territory to Him, He was able to bless me in increasing measure.

Sometimes I wondered if Jerry would be able to see the change in me. When he came home, would he notice how I'd grown spiritually? What would our life together be like? Would he be able to see the person I'd become? Slowly I came to realize that he couldn't avoid seeing the changes in me.

Somehow I concluded over the months of separation that since God had filled both Jerry and me with the Holy Spirit, He must be planning to use us in full-time Christian ministry. We'd be soon getting out of the Army. Surely God couldn't use us in the military any longer—*or could He?*

15

Chain Reaction

He told them, "The harvest is plentiful, but the workers are few.
Ask the Lord of the harvest, therefore,
to send out workers into his harvest field. Go!"
—Luke 10:2–3, NIV

Six months into his second year in Vietnam, Jerry was allowed a two-week R & R, and his joyous letter said things seemed to be working out for him to spend it with us in Colorado Springs. What great news! The excitement among the children and me and was so great that it could have been measured on a bathroom scale.

One bright and beautiful Colorado day we drove out to the airport to pick Jerry up. He was a wonderful sight for all our eyes. He had lost quite a bit of weight, but his smile was as wide as the Mississippi River. One by one he swept us up into his arms and whirled us around.

On the way home we all talked at once. The conversation wasn't very coherent, but that didn't matter. We were so happy to be together that words were inadequate to express our joy no matter what was said.

As a bit of icing on the cake, we received a phone call from Mom Curry in McKeesport saying that Jerry's younger brother Bob and his wife Joan, who were working as missionaries in Brazil, had just flown in and that they were piling into the car and driving out to visit with us in Colorado Springs before Jerry headed back to Vietnam.

Oh, and Jerry's youngest brother David was also coming along and would help with the driving. A week later they pulled into the driveway and we celebrated Jerry's joyous homecoming all over again.

In addition to hugs, kisses and family dinners, there was much prayer and Mom Curry led us in a number of Bible studies. Late one evening Bob shared how badly he and Joan wanted children. They had been married for some years and Joan had been pregnant numerous times only to miscarry or have a stillborn child. It seemed the two of them would never have children of their own.

One evening, a few days after they'd arrived in Colorado Springs and after the children had been tucked into bed, Bob said that somehow he felt this was to be the year when he and Joan would be blessed with a child.

Without thinking, Jerry suddenly said with authority, "Yes, Bob, I agree with you and the baby will be born on the 27th of November!"

Bob and Joan jumped to their feet, skipped around the small living room and clapped their hands: "The 27th of November," they kept repeating.

The rest of us didn't quite know what to make of their exuberance, but we wished them well. They left the next day and the day after that we put Jerry on a plane to wing his way back to the war in Vietnam. We didn't know it at the time, but he was flying into the mouth of the storm. His last six months there would be a time of great stress and danger.

Bob and Joan had gone to Canada to fulfill an extensive series of speaking engagements. So all across Canada audiences were told that God had promised to bless with them with a baby on the 27th of November!

When they returned to Brazil they continued to spread the message, which by now was called a prophecy. Midsummer came and Joan wasn't pregnant. August and September scrolled by with no change, but Bob and Joan were still telling people that in November they would be parents.

Their house was located in a small village in a very rural area where Bob pastored. Everyone knew everyone else and little happened that didn't immediately become public knowledge.

It was the custom there, as in many countries, to barter instead of exchange money, and often the local families showed Bob and Joan their appreciation by giving them produce or a chicken or a pig.

Early one morning Bob heard noises out on the porch. Hastily getting dressed, he went out to investigate the commotion and found that someone had left them a crate of oranges. So he picked up the crate, brought it back into the house and placed it on the kitchen table.

When he opened it up, instead of fruit he found a soundly sleeping newborn baby, only a few hours old. Pinned to her blanket was a note saying: "Please accept this baby girl as a gift from God."

"Wake up, Joan!" Bob called into the bedroom. "Wake up and see what God has done for us! He has blessed us with a baby girl!"

Joan's eyes opened and in a fraction of a second she had streaked into the kitchen and swooped up the newborn baby, blanket and all, and started cooing over her.

It took awhile, but eventually normalcy returned to the Bob Curry household. "Joan," Bob inquired, "What day is it?"

Still holding her new baby in her arms, she went into the other room, located a calendar and called back to Bob: "It's the 27th of November!"

They had people check throughout the area and with all the local midwives to locate the birth parents, but were unable. There were no missing newborns. All pregnancies were accounted for, and in a small rural area someone would know if a woman had given birth.

Bob and Joan reported to the authorities at the local courthouse what had happened and asked to adopt the baby. The clerk pointed out that adoption was impossible since the birth parents could not be located to sign the adoption papers.

Then the clerk said that although Bob and Joan could not legally adopt the child, there was another way. If they signed the birth documents saying that they were the natural birth parents, the baby girl would be theirs. They did, and so it was that Bob and Joan legally gave birth to a baby girl on the 27th of November.

Meanwhile back in the United States, I continued to fervently pray by name for each member of our extended family. I wanted them to share in the same joy and certainty of Christ that I had come to experience. First my mother joined me in accepting Jesus as Lord and Savior of her life. Next came my younger sister, Shirley, followed by my brother Gary. Soon they too were adding their prayers to mine. Obviously George, his wife Olga, and my father couldn't hold out forever against this united onslaught of prayer.

Jerry's brother, David, had been a case in point. Ten years younger than Jerry, he had followed in their father's footsteps for years. Like his father, he had participated in all the sin he could find. In fact, he invented some of his own when the natural supply ran out. Always into something, he had enlisted in the Army as a private, turned down an officer's commission but completed paramedic school, and served with the airborne in the United States and Vietnam.

He was twice shot down by the Viet Cong while flying helicopter medical evacuation missions. The large red crosses painted on the side of the helicopters were supposed to give immunity from enemy fire, but the enemy didn't seem to notice them.

On one occasion, his assault helicopter had taken a nosedive into the murky waters of the South China Sea. He ended up having to swim to shore, towing one of the crew who had been wounded and couldn't make it to shore on his own. David's Eagle Scout lifesaving merit badge came in handy. Some angel must have been looking out for him because he survived that tour, then did a tour in Europe followed by a second tour in Vietnam. As David says, he "kept at it until he got it right."

After David's discharge from the Army, he was restless—a chain smoker, a heavy drinker, and in general a problem to everyone. The members of Mom Curry's church continually prayed for him. As I recall Mom's prayers, they were along the line of asking God to bring David to a place where he would be ready to surrender his life to him, and she didn't care how God did it.

The crisis resolved itself one Saturday night when Mom invited Dave to go with her to a church meeting featuring a well-known evangelist. Finally, just to get mom "off his case," David agreed to go, but for "just this one time."

By the time the meeting was over, David had confessed his sins to God and given his life and future over to Him. David walked out of the church door a Christian, forever delivered from his addiction to nicotine and alcohol.

Almost immediately, he succumbed to two new addictions— reading the Bible, literally devouring it; and praying every possible moment. He prayed from late at night when he got out of bed to leave for his job as night nurse in the infirmary of a big steel foundry, until midday when he fell asleep with words of prayer, thanksgiving, and praise on his lips.

On the Sunday following his conversion, David walked to the front of Mom's church with a Bible in his hand. He told the congregation that he had been "born-again," filled with the Holy Spirit, and delivered from addiction to nicotine.

The church congregation was shocked. Because David had been baptized in the church when he was four years old, and because he had been a more or less regular church-goer since then even when living quite a sinful life, they all assumed that he was saved and that God was happy with him and that he was already filled with the Holy Spirit.

Now they didn't know what to make of his declaration. As time went on, David's changed lifestyle was so noticeable that the church members who had known the "Old Dave" were greatly impressed.

Some wagged their heads and said it wouldn't last, and their heads were still wagging in January when David announced that God had called him into the ministry. On February 23rd, he was scheduled to preach his first sermon. Young David Curry was traveling faster down the road of Christian growth than he had previously traveled in any other direction.

With Mom Curry in the congregation lending her unceasing prayer support, David preached so powerfully that many streamed forward when he gave the altar call. Some surrendered their lives to Jesus for the first time; others rededicated their lives to living for Christ.

Of the first to come forward for prayer, three were an answer to my personal prayers: my mother; my brother, Gary; and my baby sister, Shirley. Brother George and his wife Olga had elected not to come to the meeting.

After the service was over, people hardly knew what to think. Some were greatly disturbed by David's sermon, especially the part that said God wanted to fill everyone with His Holy Spirit, and some were not sure that God could be so real and personal as described. But many did not resist the moving of the Spirit, and were themselves set on fire with a new zeal to live for God and do God's will.

Charles Cooper, my father, had always considered himself a Christian because he had joined the church. When his conduct was measured against his peers, he scored quite well.

"If they can make it into heaven, then surely I can, too," he told us and God. But whenever he heard a sermon that said anything about repentance from sins, or being born-again or filled with the Holy Spirit, he felt uncomfortable.

Then he began to question skeptically, just as Nicodemus had done centuries before him, "I'm a sixty-year-old man! How can I be born-again? There's no sense in that, no way it can happen. I don't understand it and I don't need it."

At the same time he complained that God had failed to answer his prayers when the prayers of others around him were answered. The questions he had first asked at the time of his close brush with death in the spring of 1970 started coming up again.

He became more troubled. Whereas before he had been merely curious, now his questions were taking on a sense of weightiness that merited serious answers.

When a well-known Christian teacher came to Pittsburgh to hold a series of meetings, Mom persuaded Dad to take her to hear the speaker.

Two sermons were enough. Dad realized that being a church member didn't make him a Christian. It simply made him a church member. He came to realize that something had to happen personally between him and God to usher him into the kingdom of God. So he took action to correct the situation.

When Mom called to tell me the exciting news, I could visualize the joyous smile on her face and the sparkling tears of happiness in her warm brown eyes. My father, Charles Cooper, had joined the rest of his family in becoming part of God's family.

In November 1971, at a meeting of Christian women, Olga was added to the fold. With the insistent fervency of her prayers added to those of the rest of the family, George's days as a pagan were running out. He avoided me and the rest of the family—and God—for as long as he could. But we kept praying and the "Hound of Heaven" refused to relent.

In April of 1973, George Cooper joined the rest of us. He pulled off alongside a local road in his pickup truck, confessed his sins to God, asked for forgiveness, and invited Jesus Christ to be the Lord of his life.

It was not too long after his conversion that God began to stir up George's spirit. Soon he began to understand that God was calling him into the ministry. After his studies were completed, he was ordained a minister in the African Methodist Episcopal Church.

For three years, I had believed in my heart and prayed daily that all members of our extended family would become part of the spiritual family of God. I wasn't going to stop praying until it happened. I knew that if I faithfully did my part as in Mark 11:24, God would be faithful to do His part and draw them all into His kingdom.

I wanted more for them than to just come into the kingdom, though this was the essential first step, I wanted them to grow as Christians. What happened after they became part of God's spiritual family was most significant. For as the Bible says, "faith without works is dead." And while good works will not get you into God's family, it does demonstrate that you have indeed become a family member in good standing.

Throughout my childhood visits to our garden on Jesse Curry's little farm, Jerry's father had remained an enigma. Named Jesse for the father of King David of the tribe of Judah—the tribe of government and kingship whose name literally meant "Praise to God"—and named Aaron for the first high priest of Israel, Jesse Aaron should have signified a spiritual merging of the roles of priesthood and godly government. But instead of exemplifying those things, Jerry's father fought against God at every opportunity. Although I had never seen him in anything other than circumspect behavior when I visited his house, I knew his reputation was that of "chief sinner" of the town, while Mom Curry was thought of as "chief saint."

Small of stature, he nevertheless had more physical strength then men twice his size. Extremely proud and hard-working, and with a variety of skills seldom found in one person, he was a steel worker, farmer, brick mason, jackleg plumber and electrician. Although he lacked much in the way of formal education, he had a keen mind and a ready wit.

Jerry claimed that his father's example of hard work was a major formative influence in his own life, and that he had learned many good things from his father—including how not to follow his father's example.

Jesse was so talented, clever and industrious that he set a high standard that most men would do well to emulate. But gradually over many years his stops at the local "beer garden" for a beer on the way home from work increased to two beers, to three.

Daily drinking didn't seem to affect his work or behavior. It was the binges that finally got him. He would disappear for a day or a weekend. After each binge, it took longer and longer for him to recover.

Mom Curry prayed, we all prayed, even our children prayed for the health and recovery of Granddad Curry. In addition, many friends and church congregations also joined in prayer. There is a paraphrase in the *Living Bible* that asks whether you have ever moved the hands of God by prayer. Jesse Curry was a specific case in point and God's hands were about to move.

About eleven o'clock one night in 1972, Jesse came weaving home after a three-day binge. He almost fell through the front door, but somehow managed to wobble across the room and collapse onto the couch.

Mom Curry heard heard his car in the driveway, and then she had heard the front door open. When she pulled on her robe and walked into the neat living room and saw him, she was sorry he had come home.

His eyes were glazed, clothes filthy and reeking of alcohol and across the gray stubble on his chin drooled a trickle of tobacco spittle. Everything decent in her wanted to shove him out onto the street and to slam the door on him forever.

Revulsion overwhelmed her as she stood in the doorway looking at the once proud, brave, hard-working man who was the father of her children. Then deep inside, she said it was as if the Lord himself was speaking to her.

"Do you love him?"

"Love him? I hate him! Look at him!" Fighting nausea, she sensed the question coming again.

"Do you love him?"

"My Lord and my God, there's no way in the world anyone could love him in this drunken condition."

I don't know everything the Lord impressed upon Mom Curry that night, and I don't know everything she prayed, but together she and the Lord wrestled over her husband's place in eternity. Mom had been praying for Jesse for forty years, but never with the feverish intensity she prayed that night.

About two o'clock in the morning, when she was almost ready to give up, she sensed the Lord saying to her: "If Jesse Curry were the only person in the world, in the very condition he is in right now, I would still send my Son Jesus and He would still die for him. Don't you, his wife, love him as much as My Son and I do?"

Somewhere around three o'clock in the morning, she looked again at the wreck of the once proud Jesse Curry and by some miraculous, mysterious work of the Holy Spirit, all the hate drained out of her. The despising and revulsion were gone, her spirit swept clean of it.

Softly Mom Curry cried. The she tiptoed to the bathroom and took a clean face cloth from shelves Jesse Curry had built and she had painted. She wet the cloth with cool water from the well Jesse

Curry had dug for the house he had built with his own hands, the house in which they had reared their children, nourishing them with fruit and vegetables and eggs and milk and meat produced on their own small farm.

Walking across the wooden floor Jesse Curry had hammered into place, Mom Curry dropped on her knees and washed the spittle from his face as tenderly and lovingly as she would have washed the face of a sleeping baby. From the bedroom she got a soft blanket and a pillow with a fresh pillowcase. Leaning over, she cradled her husband's head in one arm and eased the pillow under it. Then she smoothed the blanket over him as gently as she would have tucked in a little child.

Looking down at Jesse Curry, no longer with her own eyes but with the heart of Jesus who died on the cross for him and us all, she kissed him on the forehead and went to bed.

He woke up about noontime, rested, not smelling of alcohol, and without a hangover. The following day he went back to work. They never discussed what had happened, but Jesse Aaron Curry never drank again. He remained sober for the rest of his life.

A few months later, Jerry had the priceless privilege of praying with his father to receive Jesus Christ as his healer, Savior and Lord. What a witness his new life became to the community.

16

I Can Do It!

*Also I heard the voice of the Lord, saying, "Whom shall I send, and
who will go for us?" Then said I, "Here am I; send me."*
—Isaiah 6:8, KJV
*"Therefore go and make disciples of all nations, baptizing them
in the name of the Father and of the Son and of the Holy Spirit,
and teaching them to obey everything I have commanded you.
And surely I am with you always, to the very end of the age."*
—Matthew 28:19–20, NIV

Once my family and Jerry's became part of the extended spiritual family of Christ, God's blessing spread through us to friends,
neighbors, and co-workers. Daily, God used all of us in ever-widen-
ing circles. That is, when we were willing and able to handle the
assignments He sent our way!

The next assignment came from the military, though we now
believed that it was God who told the military where to assign us.
Our military orders said that it was back to Washington, D.C. for
us. Jerry was to become a systems analyst with the Department of
the Army Staff in the Office of the Assistant Vice Chief of Staff. His
department was called Planning, Programming and Budgeting.

Of course we prayed over all the details of our move including
the place where we were to live. Unbeknown to each other, Jerry,
while in Vietnam, and I, while still in Colorado Springs, had each
been sending up matching prayers about the house we wanted—big,
white, southern-mansion style, spacious, secluded, plenty of trees,
at least two fireplaces, plenty of room for horses if we chose to have

them, a good neighborhood and neighbors, a big yard, gaslights going to the road, the school bus stopping at the front door.

When the realtor drove us up to 2100 Post Road in Vienna, Virginia, we saw that the Lord had us praying for the exact details of the place he had already chosen. Not only did the house have everything we prayed for, but there were gaslights on the driveway and the school bus stopped at our mailbox.

Yet there was a hitch. The family who owned the house was returning from an overseas assignment in ten months. While the Army paid for our relocating our household from Colorado Springs to Washington, it would not pay for us to relocate within the Washington area. This meant that ten months later when we had to move, we'd have to pay for the expense of moving out of our own pocket.

Over the years as an Army officer's wife, I had adjusted to living in genteel poverty, but paying for a second move would really cut into our finances and it would take years to recover. Yet when we prayed, the answer never seem to change: "This is the house I have provided for you."

So reluctantly we rented the house. It didn't make much sense and our military friends hinted that obviously Jerry's second tour of duty in Vietnam had caused us both to lose our grip on reality. Secretly, I sometimes felt that perhaps they were right, though I kept it to myself. To make matters even worse, the whole house was filthy. The family renting it before us had almost destroyed it.

Our ten months there were filled with changes, as prayer after prayer was heard and answered, even above all we could ask or think. The Holy Spirit had to teach us, to break us away from our old ways of doing things. We later learned that the ten-month rental was one of those growing experiences God had chosen for us.

Another breakaway experience was our becoming willing to publicly share with others what God was doing in our lives and family. These "testimonials," as they were called, though a little scary at first, became great learning experiences for us.

I remember how cautiously Jerry and I began sharing our new faith in Christ. At first, both of us were quite reluctant to accept speaking engagements when the invitations began to come—Jerry because he was so busy with his military duties, I because I was terrified at the thought of standing before an audience and having to tell others the intimate details of my life.

But over time we gradually became reconciled to the idea that God intended us to share the hope of our faith in Him with others. By the end of 1976, Jerry had spoken to groups in more than half the states across the nation.

Each time he made it plain to his listeners that what God had done for us, He could do for them, because God respects all people equally. There is no one beneath His notice, and God goes to great lengths to send His laborers to places where the potential spiritual harvest is great whether that place is close at hand or far away.

For years I had thought that being born-again was a complicated process—that a lot of groundwork had to be laid, and a whole book full of Scriptures carefully digested. But a closer look at those Scriptures, combined with many personal experiences, taught me that it wasn't that way at all. God had made being born-again the simplest thing in the world.

One day Charley, a friend of Jerry's, told us a marvelous story illustrating how simple the gospel really is. Charley was working as a military adviser with a very primitive tribe in Vietnam, a tribe of almost Stone Age simplicity.

The American forces had brought in mortars and ammunition to enable the tribe to defend itself by driving off the North Vietnamese and the Viet Cong who were constantly harassing them. It was Charley's job to explain, through an interpreter, how to set up and employ the mortars.

He drove a stake in the ground, drew a line out from it, and said, "Consider this line zero degrees." He paused, and the interpreter translated.

"Now," Charley went on, "since a complete circle is 360 degrees, if the enemy was in that direction"—he stopped talking to point—"you would rotate the mortar to fire at 90 degrees. If they were over there," he stopped to point again, "you would rotate it 45 degrees . . ."

Charley continued with his simple but precise explanation, drawing lines in the dirt to show relative locations and the angle of fire involved.

Seeing the blank stares on the faces of the natives and being suddenly aware that his interpreter had fallen silent, he looked at him questioningly.

"We have a problem, Sir," the interpreter said.

"What's the problem? I'm explaining it as simply as I know how. Surely they can understand an explanation as simple as this one. And surely you can translate it for them."

"Yes, sir, but these people don't count the way we do."

"I know that, but can't you put it to them in their terms? I mean, 45 degrees is 45 degrees in any language, isn't it?"

"Not here, sir. They don't use our numbering system. The way they count is, 'one, two—many as the trees.' The number ten is called 'many as the trees' as is the number thirty or any other number larger than two.

"I can't teach them anything as complicated as 45, or even five for that matter. So you'll have to come up with another system or, to put it bluntly, they can't get to there from here." Finally Charley resolved the problem by painting the aiming stakes different colors.

In making one plan that was able to save all people, God had to come up with something universally applicable. The plan of God's salvation is so simple that the man who counts, "One, two—many as the trees," has the same opportunity to enter the kingdom of God as the man who is a professor of higher mathematics.

It is a plan that works in any language, applying equally to everybody. The only qualification is: "Believe on the Lord Jesus Christ and you shall be saved."

If we human beings had devised the plan, it would have required at least eighteen pages of instructions in fine print and myriad forms to be filled out in quadruplicate, and still very few of us would qualify for salvation. If our government had devised the plan, it would probably encompass even more bureaucratic rules, regulations, and procedures.

Another misconception I had previously labored under was the belief that a person could be saved only by walking to the front of church and kneeling at an altar after a particularly moving sermon or at some evangelistic meeting. How wrong I was! I have since seen people converted under a mind-boggling variety of circumstances, in every kind of place—in the quiet of a bedroom, driving a car, at cocktail parties, in cafeterias, or on a city sidewalk.

While both Jerry and I soon became intensely involved in Christian ministry in our local church and community, Jerry's primary focus had to be his military duties. The work hours were long and the pressures immense, but as usual he thrived under hard work and heavy pressure.

One day Jerry came home from work chuckling. At lunch that day he was with Myrl Allinder, a Marine Corps Major, and close Christian friend. As they went through the cafeteria line together, they were joined by a most unwelcome guest—Myrl's boss.

The boss was upset by something going on in their office and ranted and raved at Myrl all through the food line. Then he followed them to a table and continued his loud harangue while they tried to eat.

Seeing he wasn't going to have a chance to say anything, Jerry pulled his little New Testament from his pocket and started to read, while Myrl sat there and took the verbal abuse.

But everyone has to breathe and after a long while, when Myrl's boss stopped to catch his breath, Jerry caught the eye of the beribboned officer and asked, "Colonel, wouldn't you like Jesus to be the Lord of your life?"

Caught completely off guard, with his defenses down, he stammered, "Why, yes, I would."

It was only about 50 steps from their table to the Pentagon prayer room. Together they made the trip and Jerry and Myrl prayed with him to invite Christ into his life. A few months later, the same colonel was seated at the head table at a military prayer breakfast waiting to give his Christian testimony.

Some of the other things I learned during our stay in Washington about walking hand in hand with God through the empowerment of the Holy Spirit, I learned at the same time Jerry learned them. Other times God would bring a lesson to me first and Jerry would learn it later; of course, occasionally it was the other way around. Finding out what God's Word said to us and then learning how to apply it to real-life situations became a most exciting adventure, and still is.

I found that it's easy to talk about Christian living—loving your neighbor as yourself, being thoughtful and considerate of others, communing with God through prayer, and the reading of the Scriptures—but it is quite another thing to do it. For example, even in the middle of Christian surroundings, life provides us many opportunities to fail, or to triumph.

For example, the second chapter of Paul's letter to the Philippians admonishes us not to think of ourselves as better or more Christian than others. Mentally I could identify with that, but what did it really mean in practical terms?

Well, I found out one day when we attended a large Christian meeting in downtown Washington. There were hundreds sitting in the audience with us and we were looking forward to an informative and uplifting message. The air outside was warm and inside the people were friendly.

The speaker was a big Texan, and his talk was laced with "I" this, "I" that, and "I" the other thing. After about the 100th use of the personal, first-person pronoun, I was fed up.

When Jerry nudged me with his elbow and whispered, "Have you ever heard anyone more egotistical in your whole life?" I agreed without reflection or hesitation.

When the speaker finally shut up and sat down, and the thousands of us in the audience started streaming out of the auditorium, a distinguished, regal-looking, white-haired woman was standing in the doorway through which we were passing. As we drew near to her, she threw both hands into the air and praised God in a loud voice.

"Oh!" she exclaimed ecstatically, "Praise the Lord! We have just heard from God's prophet!"

I thought Jerry was going to choke. Outside we turned east and walked for four blocks to a cafeteria, mostly in silence. Not knowing our hearts, someone could have assumed we were prayerfully meditating on what "God's prophet" had just said to us. The truth was that Jerry and I were furious. Our inward fuming continued all through the cafeteria line and the placing of our food on the table.

When we were seated, David, Jerry's brother who had come to Washington for a visit and who had attended the meeting with us, looked at the two of us thoughtfully and then gently said, "Are you finished grumbling?"

"Yes, I guess I am," Jerry admitted. I nodded in agreement.

"But have you ever, in all your life, heard anyone as pompous, vain and overbearing as that man?" I added.

"And as conceited," Jerry volunteered.

David interrupted our mutual tirade to ask God's blessing over the meal and we began to eat. After a few forkfuls taken in silence, David looked at us and said, "May I comment for a few moments on what we've been witnessing this morning?"

I could sense that David was not too pleased with our reactions to the speaker and I also remembered that Jerry had occasionally said that his brother David had a "ministry of rebuke."

"All right, Brother, what is it?" Jerry muttered, resigned to whatever was to come.

"God didn't send that speaker here for you two," David said softly. "But there were people in that audience whose needs and backgrounds were such that they could hear the good news of the Gospel only through a man who spoke as that tall Texan spoke.

"God sent the Texan for them, not for you. And the reason God keeps using imperfect men like that is that imperfect men and women are the only kind He has to use. There are simply no others available."

I didn't like what I suspected was coming next, but suddenly I saw what I should have been doing at the meeting. Instead of just seething with indignation while the man spoke, I should have been praying.

"Instead of finding fault," David continued, "the two of you should have been sitting in the audience praying, 'Lord, use that man for great blessings today. And give us the grace not to spoil the flow of the Spirit by being overly critical. Let us not hear the things that are upsetting to us, but let us fasten onto the good things he is saying, things with which You can bless all our lives.'

"The two of you missed the whole point of the exercise, because you forgot that everything that comes across your path, is designed by God for your perfection. That has been true ever since you since you began to walk with God in the spirit of his freedom."

I knew that Jerry felt the same as me. Spiritually we both wanted to grow. But we knew the lessons would not always be easy nor comfortable nor, unfortunately, would they always sink in permanently the first time.

17

Healing Prayer

*"Silver and gold have I none; but such as I have give I thee:
In the name of Jesus Christ of Nazareth rise up and walk."*
—Acts 3:6, KJV

As we began to apply the Word of God to our lives more and more, we learned how to cooperate with God. We began to see new breakthroughs in our spiritual lives. Through many experiences, God taught us how to live freely by using the power of His name and His Word. We were given the boldness we needed to stand firm in our beliefs.

When one of the children had transgressed a rule, Jerry and I learned to sit down around the table and hold hands and pray over them. On one occasion, Charlie had gotten way out of line. Jerry prayed, asking God to forgive her and for all the children to forgive him and me for all our sins against them in the past.

As he prayed I could see something happening in Charlie. She broke out in a joyful, "Praise the Lord! Praise the Lord!"

We all knew that God had answered our prayer since praising the Lord had certainly not been her attitude when we first sat down to pray.

But it wasn't just our children that we were concerned with. In addition to community volunteer activities and our Christian church work, we felt we should reach out to troubled teenagers. So any night of the week our house would be filled with a half a dozen to two dozen young people. They played their guitars, sang, raided the refrigerator and sat around on the floor engrossed in all sorts of discussions. Occasionally Jerry or I would sit in the middle of their circle and they would grill us on our lives and how we coped with its challenges.

Occasionally some parent would call and ask if they could drop off their teenager for a few days because they were going through some particularly difficult time and nothing the parent tried seemed to be working. We always said yes and while Jerry was away working at the Pentagon, I counseled and counseled and counseled. When Jerry returned home, I asked him to relieve me. Many of these children we were able to help; some we were not, but we always gave it our best shot.

Life with Jesus at the deliberate center of our family was making a lot of difference. In the beginning, I had cold feet about bringing Him into every situation, and Jerry did, too. But the Lord began to work on us, and didn't let us back off just because we were timid.

For example, in the spring of 1972, Jerry was asked to speak to a Christian meeting in Washington, D.C. As usual, I went along with him, but this time it wasn't just speaking that God had in mind.

Upon our arrival, the president of the organization told Jerry, "When you have finished your talk, the other officers and I will pray with people who want salvation. You and your wife can pray for the people who need to be healed."

My mouth went dry and I heard Jerry swallow hard. I looked at him and he looked at me. We had often prayed for the healing of minor ailments in our children and ourselves, but neither of us had ever prayed for strangers. It was one thing to pray for our own children, but something quite different to pray face-to-face with people we did not know. Some of them were in wheelchairs. Would God perform a miracle for them just because we asked for one? We didn't know the answer to that question.

While I pondered these things, I wondered how Jerry would get us out of this mess. I was sure he would think of something clever.

To my dismay, when he finished his talk he said, "Those who want to be saved and filled with the Holy Spirit, come to the front of the room where the chapter officers will pray for you. Those who need physical healing go to the prayer room through the door in the rear of the room, and Charlene and I will meet you there."

"Honey, I'm not too sure how this is going to turn out," I heard Jerry whisper apologetically.

"I'm not either," I whispered back, "But I'm awfully glad you're the one who will be doing the praying. I'll just stand to the side and agree with you."

I thought I'd better make him aware of just how limited my role was going to be, in case he had the idea that I was going to take the lead.

Silently praying, we stood with our eyes closed, our backs to the prayer room, while people sang and sorted themselves out for prayer. When we opened our eyes and turned around, we faced a long line—maybe fifty people or more—who wanted us to pray with them.

"Lord, you're going to have to do something spectacular," I silently prayed. "You know I can't heal people and neither can Jerry!" My prayer was especially desperate because the first person in line was a man in a wheelchair. His wife whispered to us that, according the doctors, he was dying with cancer. I could see there was no hope left for him. His limbs were practically skin and bones. His head was lying weakly over on one shoulder; his eyes were rolled upwards and out of focus.

"Folks, let's all pray," I heard Jerry say and I imagine his mind was racing, as was mine, wondering what to do next. The only words that came to me were from the book of Acts: "Your sins are forgiven. Rise up and walk." But Jerry and I didn't forgive sins, at least not the last time I looked.

For a few minutes, everyone prayed softly, and then I heard Jerry say forcefully what I had just been thinking: "As the Bible says, your sins are forgiven."

It was as if a dam had broken somewhere inside of the man. With a great release tears gushed down his face. His head wobbled around to an upright position. Then Jerry said the impossible, "Okay, now it's time to get up and walk."

For a long while the man looked at Jerry. Then slowly he thrust his body to a standing position while everyone in the room gasped. Then he took several steps forward. Suddenly I felt weak in the legs. Awestruck, we all watched the man walk stiffly out of the room. After that, I think Jerry and I had the faith to pray for anything. When Jerry suggested we divide the rest of the prayer line in two, letting me pray for some while he prayed for others, I agreed without protest. Clearly God had something He wanted to accomplish that day and He didn't care who did the praying.

One of the persons who came to me for prayer was a woman with a lump in her breast that had been diagnosed to be cancerous. She was scheduled for surgery the following week, but had come to the meeting, hoping against hope that God would do something marvelous for her.

Very calmly, I put my hands on her and prayed a simple prayer, "Father, I know it's not my prayer that heals, but your power. In the name of Jesus, I pray that the malignancy in this breast will disappear."

About a week after the meeting, the woman for whom I had prayed telephoned Jerry's office at the Pentagon. Reminding him that I had prayed for her, she gave him a message for me: "I've been back to the doctor. The lump is gone!"

A few years later at a Christian meeting in Indianapolis, Indiana, a man approached me and said, "You don't know me. But I was in Washington, D.C., when Jerry prayed for a fellow in a wheelchair. The man got up and walked off under his own steam.

"Well," the man went on, "I was the one who was pushing his wheelchair. You may not have noticed but there was a lady kneeling next to the wheelchair. When my friend stood up and walked, I cried so hard that my tears soaked the top of that lady's head. That got us acquainted. We started dating and not long afterward got married and we are still married today.

"Before the meeting, my future wife had been convinced that things like this were rigged. She got right next to the wheelchair so she could see what was happening. But you two looked too scared to have rigged anything.

"When my friend stood and walked out pushing his own wheelchair, his wife and I followed. So did my future wife who kept grilling us all the way to the car. Finally, we convinced her that his healing was, in fact, a miracle."

Perhaps that day in Washington, D.C., God knew that Jerry and I needed something tangible, something special to get us started in praying for other people. Or maybe God was just showing us that He will answer our prayers in spite of our doubts, frailties and imperfections.

Truly the Lord worked wonders that day, not just in healing afflicted people, but in reinforcing our belief that the miracles that Jesus did when He walked the earth still happen today, just as described in His Word. God's Word is for all Christians as much today as when Jesus walked the earth.

18

Eagles and Sparrows

*Your commandments give me understanding; no
wonder I hate every false way of life. Your word is a lamp
for my feet and a light for my path. I've promised it once, and I'll
promise again: I will obey your wonderful laws.
—Psalm 119:104–106, NLT*

For the United States, but most especially for military families like ours, the 1970s were exceedingly difficult years. Our loved ones, like Jerry, were far away in Vietnam risking their lives carrying out the nation's policies; yet back at home these same military men and women were being blamed for our nation's ills.

I could understand why someone might be opposed to the War in Vietnam. In every war there are good, decent people who are legitimately opposed to it for one reason or another—there is nothing new there. Even in the Revolutionary War, many American colonists were opposed to it. General George Washington was not overwhelmed with citizen support that bitter winter he and his soldiers spent at Valley Forge, Pennsylvania.

But what I did not understand is why college presidents and faculty members, especially those at Ivy League colleges, turned against the military servants of our nation. I could not understand why they condemned those faithful young men and women who were paying for America's freedom of speech with their lives in far-off Southeast Asia.

I found the words and actions of some U.S. congressmen and clergy particularly offensive and misguided. They, of all people, should have known better. For example, instead of insisting that military recruiters and ROTC be driven off college campuses and forbidden in high schools, they should have used the opportunity to teach our youth an important civics lesson.

The college students should have learned that it's wrong to spit on or demean those who carry out the policies of the nation's government, which the citizens themselves have elected, just because you don't agree with the government's policy. They should have been taught to direct their energy and efforts toward changing the minds of those who made the policy, or toward changing the government itself. Our college youth should have been taught that no one in the military has the power to change governmental policy. Only our civilian leaders have that power, thank God.

Few of our young people learned in college that demonstrations should be directed toward the President and the U.S. Congress, not against the lowly soldiers, sailors and airmen who were risking their lives daily to advance the cause of freedom. In short, during this period of time many of the nation's colleges and universities failed us and our children, especially the Ivy League colleges.

For freedom's sake, the nation needs military leaders who hear a different drummer, who are not part of a military aristocracy, who are willing to internally take a different view, or, perhaps, express a non-traditional opinion. The more diverse those are who enter the military and make it a career, including college students, the safer our great democracy will be.

Men and women from schools like Harvard, Yale, UCLA and Kent State should be a wonderful protection against the politicization or misuse of military power. Shouldn't these colleges and universities be welcoming ROTC to their campuses as well as recruiters from all branches of the government?

It was during this twilight time that something unusual happened in our family. It began with a fast. Throughout the Bible various leaders fasted for spiritual guidance. From Moses to Daniel to Jesus Christ the Son of God to Saint Paul, all experienced prolonged fasts.

Both Jerry and I had fasted in various ways and for different lengths of time over the years, and so it was not that unusual when one day Jerry said, "I think I'm going to be fasting next week. No solid food, just liquids like soup and juice."

At the end of that week he said, "It seems to me that I need to continue on with this fast." And so he did. Of course he continued to work every day and never told anyone other than me what he was doing.

While these changes were taking place in us and our children, significant changes were also taking place in America. And the nation would never be quite the same.

In the early hours of June 17, 1972, five men broke into the Democratic National Committee Headquarters at the Watergate complex in Washington, D.C. The Watergate was a rambling group of buildings spread over ten acres of prime real estate that included fashionable offices and shops, a hotel, and apartment buildings.

The men apprehended included an ex-CIA employee, three Cubans from Miami, and James McCord. McCord worked for the Committee to Reelect President Nixon. The President of the United States had, unknowingly, become involved in a criminal break-in and burglary.

The political malignancy on the presidency grew and festered until it was recognized as terminal. As a result, President Nixon was compelled to resign from office on August 9, 1974.

* * *

During this time of major national instability, our focus was nevertheless on our family and learning how to be more effective parents to our children. Instead of harping on their shortcomings as we had in the past, punishing them for their mistakes and letting it go at that, we began to see that we needed to learn how to help them grow in the right direction.

One night Butch arrived home late after an evening out with a neighborhood friend. When he came over to my chair to kiss me goodnight, he apparently forgot that I have a super-keen sense of smell and could detect immediately what he had been up to. No matter how many bottles of mouthwash he had used to try to disguise it, he was still reeking of cigarettes and beer.

The issues here were much broader and more important than beer and cigarettes. Of course I was concerned about the physical damage smoking could do to a young body. But then there was also the fact that Butch had broken the law. At his age the purchase of neither cigarettes nor beer was lawful. Somehow he and his friend had circumvented the law and if reported, there would be a penalty not only for them but for the adult who made their illegal act possible as well.

Finally, and most importantly, there was the consideration of having been disobedient to the rules of the family. Butch knew full well that Jerry and I forbade all of our children to drink and smoke.

Since Jerry was at home, I let him handle the situation. I had more than handled my share of them when he was away in Vietnam.

So when Jerry ordered Butch to go to his room and followed him, I knew he was in for it. Jerry was a strict, no-nonsense disciplinarian and I could see him in my mind's eye taking off his belt as he had done many times in the past. I prayed the physical punishment would accomplish its purpose.

But I didn't hear the door close behind them, and I could still hear voices coming down the hallway. Jerry was explaining to our son that this was more than a physical problem, it was also a spiritual battle.

"Your mother and I have set down clear rules for you to follow," Jerry began. "But it seems none of these things have made the necessary impact on your behavior. Sometimes I feel that all we've done is make you more rebellious than you might have been if we had let you alone.

"Son, I love you and your mother loves you. But you're no longer just my problem. You are also God's problem. And now God is going to have to deal with you."

The old Jerry would long since have finished Butch's spanking and a chastened son with a sore backside would be sobbing in his bedroom. I couldn't help overhearing as Jerry read our son some pertinent Bible passages from the Book of Proverbs and then prayed over him. Butch responded by running to the bathroom and losing all the contents of his stomach.

Then Jerry explained that in life there are essentially two kinds of people—sparrows and eagles. Every person has to make up his own mind as to which he chooses to be. "Sparrows" flock together, trying to please their peers, a habit that invariably leads to the perpetuation of the lowest common denominator among them. An "eagle," on the other hand, chooses to stand alone, above the common flock, in order to follow the highest calling God has for him.

Most analogies break down under close scrutiny, but for Butch, that night, this one was perfect. Young Jerry seemed to pride himself on being an underachiever, being part of a generation that had for its motto, "If you'll feed me, I'll sleep for it."

Jerry and I had grown up knowing that there is no such thing as a free lunch, that someone always has to pick up the tab. We knew that if we were ever going to have anything, we'd have to work for it, just as our parents had done before us. We had seen that success in one's chosen profession wasn't to be had by simply going another round on the golf course. Success depended on grueling hard work. Jerry had seen that in his father, Jesse. Jesse hadn't wished his house onto the acreage he had bought. He had taken hammer and saw, bricks and mortar, and put the house together with blood, sweat, and tears.

There were enough helping hands from his wife and children that they, too, knew the house didn't just grow there on that plot of land. Jerry and I had learned that the vegetables that came in such abundant profusion from the garden didn't appear mysteriously overnight. Seeds were planted, the young plants were weeded and watered, the soil was kept loose with hoeing, and the beans were picked and washed and shelled and cooked before they appeared on the table. The example of Jerry's parents' hard work was ever before him. Many nights I had seen my own father come home tired and exhausted from his day of work in the mines.

Months later, on September seventh, it was Jerry's birthday and we all enjoyed a birthday feast together. That is, everyone except Jerry, who was fasting. The girls were clearing the table while I was beginning to serve the tall chocolate cake with seven-minute icing, putting the slices on the sparkling crystal plates that were stacked before me. I had just picked up the ice cream scoop to add the ice cream topping to his piece of cake when Butch asked to be excused from the table. He would be back in just a minute, he said.

When he returned, he was carrying his guitar. "Happy birthday, Dad," he said. "I have a present for you." Then he sat and played while he sang an original composition of his own, a soul-searching song about how good it was when the son of an eagle had finally decided that he too would be an eagle and not a sparrow.

When our time in Washington was up, the movers drove away with our household goods, and we swept up the debris and locked the door on the empty house in Vienna. It had been a great ten months and we would miss the neighbors and the neighborhood.

When we arrived at our new house at the U.S. Army War College in Carlisle Barracks, Pennsylvania, Jerry decided that God no longer wanted him to continue fasting.

It had been forty days since he'd eaten his last solid meal and he had lost a lot of weight, but otherwise he was doing fine. Even though medical doctors say it shouldn't be done after a long fast, his first meal was spaghetti, meatballs, and garlic bread. He certainly ate as though he hadn't eaten for forty days!

19

To Stay or Not to Stay

You must accept whatever situation the Lord has put you in,
and continue on as you were when God first called you.
This is my rule for all the churches.
—1 Corinthians 7:17, NLT

W hile we were learning to walk with the Lord in a new, exciting way, there was a growing need to face the question that comes eventually to every military officer and his family. Should we get out of the service while Jerry was still young enough to get established in another career? Or should we stay in?

We both knew that because Jerry was an ex-enlisted man, it was unlikely that he would be promoted much above his present rank of Lieutenant Colonel. Historically those with enlisted backgrounds seldom scaled the heights of the military. It was not a prejudice against people like Jerry, it was just that West Point officers were better trained and prepared to be officers than graduates of Officer Candidate School. And to my thinking they should be, or else the nation had wasted an awful lot of taxpayer money educating them.

One night, Jerry decided to call the whole family together for a top-level conference. The children joined us around the Duncan Phyfe dining table, now in bad need of refinishing after all its many traumatic journeys halfway around the world and back. It was time to consider our options, and discuss the advantages and disadvantages of each. We had been talking about all the pros and cons of army life for months and felt that the time had come to make a decision.

Jerry explained to the children that he, as a lieutenant colonel with twenty years of service behind him, could retire from the Army and take up another career. Then we could spend our lives together instead of apart so much of the time.

He reminded them of how he had entered the service as a very green young private, with no special background to recommend him either from family status or education. Maybe he could now be an administrator in a Christian organization, or do some other Christian work where we could all be with him most of the time.

After the children had explained their feelings about staying or getting out of the Army, Jerry prayed for all of us, "Father, You see that we don't care whether we remain in the military or get out of it. We want only to do Your will, and You're going to have to give us a sign to show us unmistakably what Your will is in this matter, or we'll be guaranteed to miss it."

My own prayers that night were more internal than expressed, because I was hesitant to voice them aloud. If God had been reading the desires of my heart, however, He'd have seen something like this:

"Lord, you know that I'm tired of being both mother and father to all these children while Jerry is away for months at a time. Besides, the new spiritual life you have shown Jerry and me—together—is fantastic. But I don't think it will be possible for us to live the kind of life you want us to live if we stay in the military . . ."

Even though I had come to know the Lord in a new way, and was experiencing God's presence during Jerry's prolonged absences in a new way, the children and I still didn't like him to be an absentee father so much of the time. And Jerry was quite aware of the difficulties his long absences created for us. He didn't like being away from his family either, especially now that we were spiritually one, living our lives for God.

I was expecting the Lord to move us out of military life with record-breaking speed. The answer to our collective prayer that night which expressed a desire to do God's will, whatever that was, was on the way.

The first part of the answer came in the form of an unexpected change of status. We had expected to be in the Washington, D.C. area at least three years, the usual length of time for a Pentagon assignment. A month after our prayer, Jerry was walking down one of those Pentagon halls when a major came up to him and said, "Congratulations, Sir. I see that you are on the promotion list."

"You're mistaken," Jerry told him. "I just got here. Besides, as you know there are certain qualifications for promotion, and I don't have them at this time. I'm not in the zone for promotion."

"I don't know about all that, Sir. I just know that your name is on the list for promotion to full colonel."

Jerry hadn't even read the list, because he knew he wasn't eligible to move up. But after his encounter with the major, he checked it out. Sure enough, his name was there along with his serial number. But how could that be? He hadn't been a lieutenant colonel long enough to be considered for promotion.

So Jerry phoned his good friend, Big John McCleod, who was in personnel. "That's right, Jerry. We picked you. You're on the list. I know you're below the zone of promotion, but that doesn't matter. For promotion we're allowed to choose five percent of the most outstanding lieutenant colonels in the Army from below the zone of normal consideration. You made the cut and you deserve it."

Later, we would learn that Jerry's selection was primarily because of his outstanding war record.

In another month, another list came out—this one with the names of the officers who were assigned to attend the Army War College in Carlisle, Pennsylvania, a necessary first step for men who were on their way to becoming general officers. Jerry's name was on this second list, meaning he'd have the opportunity to study such subjects as military strategy, national and international affairs, economics, and political science, and how our government works at the national level.

Essentially the War College is the military equivalent of a Ph.D. If you aren't selected to attend the War College, it is doubtful whether you'll ever be considered for promotion to general.

Now we'd once again be able to spend time in an academic setting with other families as well as with top-level civilians from the State Department, CIA, and other governmental agencies. Wives were permitted to attend some of the lectures, and I planned to take full advantage of the opportunity to further my own education. It was a fringe benefit for which I was grateful.

We'd asked God to take us out of the Army if it was His will, and He was showing us that He intended that we remain on active duty. It wasn't the answer we were looking for, but it didn't matter. We wanted to do God's will.

Of course this meant that once more I'd be packing up the family, bag and baggage, and moving us to a new city and a new house. While I really enjoyed army life—family separations excepted—there were also some glaring disadvantages.

For example, I cringed at the memory of all the occasions when I had polished our quarters to the hilt for required parties for the commanders and junior officers who served under Jerry, all the silver gleaming, the crystal sparkling, every budget-breaking hors d'oeuvre a work of art, not a piece of furniture that hadn't been highly polished—and I had left my children neglected in the kitchen while I acted the part of charming hostess in the living room among all the splendid uniforms and evening dresses.

Further signs of a rapid rise through the ranks were fast in coming when we got to Carlisle. Midway through the War College year, Jerry's name appeared on the first command list. He had been selected to be a brigade commander. Graduating from the War College on June 11, 1973, Colonel Hal Barber (the college's chief of staff) and I pinned the silver eagles on Jerry's uniform. Once-upon-a-time Eagle Scout Jerry Curry was now Colonel Jerry Curry!

Standing there beside the American flag, my heart filled with wifely pride at Jerry's accomplishments. Somehow, I knew this wasn't the last step. The old game we used to play, speculating and laughing about the improbability of his being promoted to general officer someday, wasn't a game anymore. Being a general was now only one step away.

Turning my mind back to the evening when our children had sat around the table and prayed about Jerry's career, giving the whole matter thoroughly into the hands of the Lord, I saw that He had indeed taken over, and given it back to us multiplied many times over.

There was no question in my mind about whether or not a military man could walk with the Lord. In the Bible book of Genesis, God's high priest, Melchizedek, had blessed Abraham for fighting and winning a war. In the book of Revelation, Michael and his angels fight a war against Satan and his angels. Finally, Jesus himself is designated to be the commander-in-chief of the last army to fight on earth.

Throughout the history of the Jews, God used war as an instrument to accomplish His divine purpose, whenever His divine wisdom required it, and gave victories to the armies that did His will. Could a Christian be a career military man? Absolutely.

20

A Word of Life

And we know that in all things God works for the good of those who love him, who have been called according to his purpose.
–Romans 8:28, NIV

Now that our decision was made to stay in the Army, the Lord confirmed the rightness of our choice. But all was not sweetness and light. It never is. Life is full of trials and conflict.

This particular "trial" began when a group of army chaplains, Jerry's fellow War College students, asked the chief of staff, Colonel Hal Barber, for permission to talk to the commanding general.

When Hal asked what they wanted to discuss with General Davis, they told him that Jerry and I were religious fanatics and that they felt we were corrupting the children of the students and faculty by forcing our radical religious views on the other War College families. In their minds we were a clear and present danger to the military community. The answer they proposed was to have Jerry dismissed from the War College and involuntarily retired from the Army.

Hal told me that he heard them out, and then told them that he and his family had gotten to know our family well. They found us to be dedicated Christians with strong convictions, not religious fanatics. It seemed to him that the student officers, particularly chaplains, would do well to examine themselves and their motives. Then he closed the discussion by telling them that from time to time his family and ours had prayed together and, "What did they find objectionable in that?"

At this, the chaplains tucked their tails between their legs and skulked off.

The year at Carlisle was a time of great family togetherness and a wonderful opportunity to meet and get to know many of our peers with whom we would work and socialize throughout the remainder of our active army days. Many of them joined us in skiing at Pennsylvania's Roundtop ski slopes. It wasn't the same as skiing the Austrian Alps, but it made for a lot of family togetherness and fun.

Unfortunately one day I became a little too aggressive in my skiing and ended up with a broken leg. The cast ran from the bottom of my foot almost to the groin. It was months before they cut the cast off and I could once again walk without hobbling.

Since Pennsylvania was our home of record, it was financially convenient for our oldest daughter, Charlie, to take a full load of classes at Harrisburg Community College. It was only about a half hour drive each way. This worked out exceptionally well. She was still able to live at home and daily drive her Volkswagen "Bug" into Harrisburg for classes. We were an exceptionally tight family, and we enjoyed having her at home that extra year as much as she enjoyed being home with us.

Charlie was not one who liked academics, though she was a good student. One day while attending the sixth grade she had come home and announced that she had decided to quit school because it bored her. It took a lot of talking but, with Jerry's help, I was able to get her to stick it out until the end of the school year.

After that, at least once during each of the following school years she would say to me something to the effect of, "School is just not my thing and the sooner I can stop going to school the better."

And each year I was again successful in encouraging her to "Hang in there and do the best you can." She did.

But when she finished high school, it really got serious, and more and more I had to call in Jerry for reinforcement.

Charlie said that what really got to her was one day when I asked her, "What standard of living do you want in life?"

"Well," she had answered, "I want to live at least as well as you and Dad do, perhaps a little better."

"Can you afford to live like that on a waitress' pay? Because without a college education, that's the kind of job you'll probably have to settle for."

Charlie was not happy with the way this conversation was going and tried to slip out from under its implications, but I wouldn't let her.

"Well," she countered, "my husband will be able to afford it."

"Charlie, do you think a man who earns that much money will be a college graduate?"

"Oh, yes," she quickly replied. For a minute she pondered my question and her response.

Then her happy countenance changed to sadness. She dropped her head and mumbled, "He'd probably want a wife who had at least some college, wouldn't he?"

Later she said it was a throwaway line I'd used that finally pushed her over the line. I had said, "Charlie, you're going to have to eat a lot of beans to live as well as Dad and I live." Charlie hated beans.

She had always been very goal-oriented and now she realized that reaching her goals and achieving her desired standard of living would require a college education.

She saw the wisdom in what we had been saying, so she assigned college to the place in her head titled, "One more of life's challenges to be overcome." When Charlie set a goal, it was as good as achieved. Soon she was enrolled at Harrisburg Junior College.

She recognized that when our family's year at Carlisle came to a close, she would have to enroll in a four-year college somewhere. So she and Jerry spent the better part of a month trying to find a curriculum that appealed to her.

Finally, she settled on Dental Hygiene. Then the question became, to which colleges should she apply? Together she and Jerry sat at the kitchen table and poured through a stack of college catalogs. Charlie unenthusiastically applied to several colleges. One was in South Dakota. Don't ask me how that happened, I don't remember. Maybe it was by osmosis.

One day Jerry and I drove her to the Harrisburg airport and put her on a plane. After being interviewed by the University of South Dakota (USD), she flew back home to us and said that while she liked the USD, and while they had been unusually kind to her, the Dental Hygiene program was oversubscribed by the locals and no out-of-state students were being accepted for the next year.

So it was somewhat of a shock when a few months later a letter arrived from USD's admissions office saying that Charlie had been accepted into the School of Dental Hygiene. After comparing and contrasting the other colleges' programs, Charlie decided to accept the USD offer.

While there, she met and fell in love with a wonderful young man from Nebraska, Raleigh Vantramp. Today she and Dr. Vantramp are married and have a very successful dental practice in Federal Way, Washington State. They have two beautiful married daughters and it is always a joy to visit them there and learn of the wonderful things God is doing in their lives, and the lives of their children. And . . . Charlie doesn't have to eat beans.

After Jerry graduated from the War College, we all packed up and for the third time headed back to Germany for another tour of duty. That is, with the exception of Charlie, who was already well established in the dorm at USD.

We were all excited at the opportunities for travel and adventure awaiting us in Europe, plus we knew there would be occasions to share our Christian faith with those who showed an interest. Had we known all the things that would happen, we might have missed our flight—deliberately. But the good things came first.

On June 29, 1973, Jerry assumed command of the Third Brigade of the Eighth Infantry Division in Mannheim, West Germany. And once again I became a First Lady. Jerry was back with his first love—commanding combat troops in the field—and so he was constantly touring the East German border, inspecting and memorizing the ground over which his brigade would have to fight, should the Russians invade West Germany.

His days were spent riding in jeeps, flying helicopters, or on foot hiking over the rugged German terrain with the infantry soldiers. He checked out artillery positions, and supervised tank gunnery, which meant training and qualifying tank crews to properly fire their weapons when engaging Russian tanks.

At the same time, God gave me an opportunity to host Monday morning Bible studies in our home. Though the group was small in the beginning, it grew both in numbers and in stature. Together we wives prayed, studied the Bible, and grew in our faith and knowledge of God. Then the ladies went home and shared with their husbands and families some of the things that they had learned that week at the study. Many households were blessed from those Monday morning Bible studies.

Our own children were also included in faith-building activities. Toni and young Jerry joined a Christian musical group, called Come Together, that toured the country singing to the GIs at different army bases and to people in the neighboring towns. It was sponsored by an organization called Youth With a Mission.

In addition to the Monday morning ladies' fellowship, Jerry and I occasionally hosted evening parties for Christian leaders in the community. Some army chaplains, such as Colonel Jim Ammerman who was then V Corps headquarters chaplain, came from other cities to join in the fellowship.

Of course the children insisted that we head out for the ski slopes as often as possible. They all progressed well and, according to a member of the Austrian national ski team, son Jerry was developing Olympic-caliber skills.

The children were all fast becoming adults and it amazed me to see how large they had grown and how very special and unique each one was. Charlie was doing great at USD. Son Jerry was in his junior year of high school. Toni had blossomed into a teenager, and young Natasha, or "Tash" as we called her, was showing her independence at every opportunity. And when an opportunity failed to present itself, she didn't hesitate to create one.

Jerry's tour as brigade commander couldn't have gone better. As did all brigade commanders in U.S. Army Europe, he faced many challenges and difficulties, but God helped him overcome them all.

His first division commander was Major General Fred Davison, who was the first African American in our nation's history given command of an army division. Fred was exceptionally competent and provided excellent leadership for us all.

After several months he rotated back to the United States and was replaced by Major General Joe McDonough. Joe and his wife provided just the right touch the division needed in those difficult and challenging days. Our nation was indeed fortunate to have had two such outstanding general officers.

And then one day it was over. Jerry passed the Third Brigade flag to another colonel and we packed up for a move to Frankfurt, Germany, where Jerry would become a member of the V Corps staff.

21

Trials

Jerry's new title was Special Assistant to the V Corps Chief of Staff. Literally interpreted it said, "He doesn't have a regular assigned job, so this is just to keep him busy until we can find or invent something for him."

For an office, he was given a sort of cubbyhole, a large closet where the German phone company had installed a phone and one of the headquarters' clerks had hung a picture to cover a telephone junction box that adorned one of his windowless walls.

The office became a sort of headquarters joke. It was a far step down from the exalted position of brigade commander. Still Jerry didn't complain; "It's a lesson in humility," he said. I felt that he deserved better. Evidently so did the Lord.

One evening we hosted a dinner at our quarters for some of the V Corps staff. I don't remember the exact menu, but the food came out perfectly and the house was polished to perfection. After dinner Lieutenant General Bill Desobry, the V Corps commander, asked that we charge our glasses and stand for a toast.

"Here's to Jerry and Charlene Curry," he offered, raising his champagne glass. "Tomorrow morning the Department of the Army will announce that Jerry has been selected to be promoted to brigadier general. Shall we all drink to the Curry's health?"

"Hear, hear!" everyone enthusiastically shouted in reply. A wonderful evening suddenly became perfect. The best part was that it was unexpected. Again Jerry had been selected for a fast promotion. He had been a full colonel for less than two years. A few months later, when the single silver star of a brigadier general was pinned on his collar, he became the youngest general officer in the Army. He had come a long way from private to corporal to second lieutenant to general. That night Jerry and I prayed and thanked God for having blessed us so much.

But there was no sense of having arrived at a final destination, no inner voice that said, "Yes, that's it. Being a general officer in the United States Army is the very special purpose for which Jerry Curry was born into the world."

Among the happy milestones during our stay in Germany was the wedding in the Frankfurt chapel of our daughter Charlie to Raleigh Vantramp. The Corps Commander's wife was Jackie Desoby, a warm, intelligent and caring woman. When she learned of the wedding, she phoned and asked me over for tea.

Then taking me by the hand she led me back into the inner reaches of the Number 10 Ditmar Strasse house where she and Bill Desobry lived, and she retrieved some packages out of storage.

"Charlene," she said, "I don't have any idea why I've kept these over the years, but if you can use them you're more than welcome."

Then out of the thick plastic zippered garment bags she pulled out and laid on the bed a complete array of dresses to outfit the entire wedding party. First there was the beautiful off-white wedding dress itself. Then bridesmaid gowns, a gorgeous celadon green.

When I got home, Charlie, Toni, and Natasha tried on the gowns and they fit perfectly, without needing alterations. This was a present from God as well as from Jackie and I profusely thanked both. So the wedding went forward without us having to pay a penny for wedding dresses.

Afterward, Charlie and Raleigh went off on a wonderful honeymoon tour of Bavaria and the Alps. Months later, a phone call from the States gave us the exciting news that our first grandchild was on the way.

One day during our stay in Frankfurt, Jerry went to a German Christian men's meeting in Stuttgart. Although it was a long drive, Jerry felt God really wanted him to go. Little did we suspect that God intended to provide great encouragement for us through that meeting. At the time we didn't know it, but God knew that a serious crisis was coming and so He was moving to prepare us for it.

The German meeting happened to coincide with the coming of a group of Americans from the United States who were traveling around the continent encouraging European Christians. About a dozen members of the group wound up at the same meeting with Jerry.

At lunchtime Jerry happened to be seated next to a doctor from Yakima, Washington. The visitor impressed upon him the importance of walking close to and trusting God, particularly when faced with making a hard decision.

"Once you have done all you know to do and all you believe God would have you do, the results of the decisions you have made are God's responsibility. The Bible says, 'Commit your way unto the Lord and He will bring it to pass.'"

Jerry was so impressed with some of the things the doctor said that he wrote them down and shared them with me after he came home.

The doctor's words confirmed to me a verse in Romans that had previously worked its way into my spirit: "And we know that all things work together for good to them that love God, to them who are the called according to His purpose" (Romans 8:28, KJV).

I thought about all the times in the past when I had agonized over my mistakes, fretted over what seemed to be wrong decisions, and worried myself nearly to death over judgments that seemed less than the best. Somehow I knew that I wouldn't do that sort of thing any more. After consulting God, I would act according to the best leading I had received from Him. Then I would trust God to make things turn out for the best.

What confidence these thoughts gave me! And what peace! In the days ahead as I studied the Bible, I found confirming verses everywhere: "Where the Spirit of the Lord is, there is liberty" (2 Cor. 3:19), and "If the Son therefore shall make you free, you shall be free indeed" (John 8:36), and "Stand fast therefore in the liberty wherewith Christ has made us free, and be not entangled again with the yoke of bondage" (Gal. 5:1). All of them reinforced each other and the feelings I had deep in my heart.

I would need their comfort because suddenly Jerry was plunged into the deepest crisis of his military career. An impossible-to-avoid confrontation with an unethical superior officer embroiled him in a situation in which he could have lost all he had worked for. He had to risk forfeiting his army career and his allegiance to the ethical standards of the United States Army.

It was almost as if the Lord had said to Satan, "Have you considered my servant, Jerry Curry?" and had subsequently removed the hedge of His divine protection from around him just as he had removed it from Job centuries before (Job 1:8). The result was that our entire family was forced into coping with some fierce realities.

I knew, and Jerry knew, that he was morally right in the stand he took, even though in military life it is considered treason for a junior officer to take a stand contrary to his superior's. But in life even when we try to do the right thing, we sometime find ourselves faced with trying times. Those darkest days for us as a family could have been filled with worry and nightmarish imaginings of what was going to happen next.

But I kept reminding God, "Lord, if the words You gave us at Stuttgart are really from You, when this is all over, it will be clear that Jerry made the right decision and followed the best course of action. He did what was right, and he is trusting You to make it come out right, for Your glory."

Five interminable months later, it was all over, and the Yakima doctor's words proved to be true. In place of all the scathing criticism Jerry had received, and utter abandonment by many he thought were his friends but who were opportunistically interested in saving their own skins, he was commended by the U.S. Army for the heroic stand he had taken. His unethical commander was demoted a grade and forced to retire.

Through all the months of trials, our faith in God never wavered. In the end we found ourselves "counting it all joy" (James 1:2-8), just as God's Word said we should. But it wasn't easy.

22

Fulfillment

"For I know the plans I have for you," declares the Lord,
"plans to prosper you and not to harm you, plans to give you hope
and a future. Then you will call upon me and come and pray
to me, and I will listen to you. You will seek me and find me
when you seek me with all your heart."
—Jeremiah 29:11–13, NIV

Skiing continued to be a family passion, but particularly for me. Unfortunately one day my ski binding released on a run down the south face of the Eiger Mountain in Austria and I took a terrible spill. I tore a ligament in my right leg and I ended up with a cast that reached to just above my right knee. It was no fun dragging my leg around like a mummy all day.

When my leg healed and the cast was cut off the doctor said, "Mrs. Curry, I've been looking at the record of your medical history and all the things you've done to your legs skiing over the years. Isn't there some other sport that might interest you?"

There was—tennis. So a few months later I persuaded Jerry to enroll the two of us in the U.S. Forces' tennis camp at Garmish. Soon my passion for skiing was transferred to the tennis court. I became an ardent tennis lover. But occasionally when I see skiers on TV, I become just a little wistful.

That winter of 1975–1976, the nation was rapidly moving toward the celebration of its bicentennial and all of us, but particularly Jerry, got swept up in the national enthusiasm. Jerry started digging through the books and notes he had accumulated during his many years of studying history. History had been one of his majors in undergraduate school and he belonged to an international historical society.

In the meantime, orders came reassigning us back to the United States. We had wanted to remain in Germany, but though Jerry was exonerated from his run in with his unethical boss, evidently the powers that be wanted him out of Europe and in some place where they could watch him more closely.

Jerry's new job was in Washington, D.C., where he became Deputy Commander of the Military District of Washington. His boss was Major General Bob Yerks. Both Bob and his wife, Iris, were wonderful Americans and we both learned a lot from them, and grew to love them and their many children.

In addition to helping Bob with his duties, which involved the celebration of the bicentennial in the nation's capital, Jerry would also be helping him prepare for the upcoming inauguration of the next president of the United States: either Jerry Ford or Jimmy Carter.

Our son, Jerry, who as a senior had remained behind in Germany so he could graduate from Frankfurt Military High School, was now back in the U.S. with us. The girls were growing and involved in all sorts of teenage activities. Toni was now in high school and Natasha was close behind her. With both Charlie and young Jerry out of the nest, we were glad that the younger girls were still with us.

It was an exciting time for all of us, and every time we turned around there seemed to be a concert, play, or musical performance of some kind celebrating our nation's bicentennial—a special at the Kennedy Center, or the Harlem Ballet performing at the Carter Barron Amphitheater, or Abe Polin's Capital Centre hosting a spectacular. Plus, all the Smithsonian Museums were in their full glory.

With all these patriotic things going on simultaneously, it was only natural that the first time I heard Jerry talk to an audience about his historical research on the spiritual roots of America, I was greatly stirred. The theme of his talk was that the Founding Fathers, though not all Christians, were guided in their actions by Christian principles as expressed in the Bible.

He said that just as it was impossible to understand an Arab nation except against the background of Islam, and just as it is impossible to understand Israel except against the background of Judaism, so it is impossible to understand the United States except against the background of Christianity. This didn't mean that the United States was founded as an entirely Christian nation, but rather that its guiding principles were built on a Christian foundation.

It was also in the bicentennial year that Jimmy Carter was elected President. On the inaugural day the following January, bitter cold numbed our feet and faces. Jerry wielded the outside edge of his hand like an axe, shattering the layered "cellophane" of ice frozen across the seats of the metal chairs, then scraped them clean with the palm of his black-gloved hand so we could sit down.

Already thousands of people were gathering. The reserved seat section in which we were sitting filled more rapidly than the aisles and the ushers could handle. Only the cold held back the stampede for seats and reserved standing room. Trying to keep warm, I banged the soles of my boots against one another beneath the West Point lap blanket that was draped over my legs.

From time to time, various people worked their way through the masses of people, nodded to me, and spoke quietly to Jerry. He agreed or disagreed with a movement of his head. They nodded to me again and left.

The United States Marine Band played. And again I stamped my numb feet. Jerry looked at his watch. I looked at mine: 11:30, January 20, 1977.

Suddenly the perfectly coached band stopped playing abruptly, as if the sound were an icicle that some giant fist had grabbed and broken off in midair. So far, everything was moving according to schedule, just as Bob Yerks and Jerry had planned it.

Diagonally in front of us, members of the House of Representatives were filing to the inaugural platform. Next came the members of the United States Senate, followed by the governors of the fifty states and the diplomatic corps. Then the President-elect's cabinet was escorted onto the Presidential platform and seated. Last came the robed justices of the U.S. Supreme Court.

Applause announced the arrival of Mrs. Ford and Mrs. Rockefeller. It increased in volume as Mrs. Carter and Mrs. Mondale entered. I noticed that Mrs. Carter was wearing a green cloth coat . . .

"How would it feel to be the First Lady of the United States of America?" I wondered.

And then came the swearing-in of Fritz Mondale, the Vice President. Finally the moment the nation and much of the world was waiting for arrived, and Jimmy Carter took the oath of office. Jerry took an advanced copy of Carter's speech from his pocket and the two of us read along with our new President.

The bicentennial and the inauguration were heady experiences for us, and the close-up exposure to places of power and leadership made my head spin. But it was also distressing to be back in the U.S. and see so much change. All around us there seemed to be a determined assault on the traditional family.

It seemed to me that at every hand our family values and morals were being publicly ridiculed, attacked or undermined, especially by the news media and some of the nation's elites.

Such unwarranted meddling sends a clear message to our children: parents need not be consulted by their children when they have to make momentous decisions with far-reaching consequences for the rest of their lives. Parents need not be consulted because the government, by its policies or lack of them, is saying that parents have no real authority or control over their children. The message being sent seems to be that the government, the schools, and the family planning/abortion clinics are the only authorities to which our children need turn for direction and guidance.

After the successful 1977 inauguration, we had a few months' respite. Then, thanks to the help Jerry received from an old friend, General Fritz Kroeson, we moved from Alexandria, Virginia to Fort Carson, Colorado. There Jerry became Assistant Division Commander of the Fourth Infantry Division.

Once more he was back with his first love, commanding troops in the field. For me there was tennis, and for the children skiing. Though they had skied all over Europe, they felt that the best powder skiing was in the Rocky Mountains, particularly the Colorado Rockies. Spring skiing was at Taos, New Mexico. Further west at Pagosa Springs, located halfway between Wolf Creek Pass and Durango, there was some of the best trout fishing in the world.

These were happy days for us as a family. All of us had favored activities and I even learned how to bake bread and cakes at high altitudes. There were always interesting things to do such as visiting deserted mining towns or the Air Force Academy. Jerry got to do quite a bit of trail riding with an old cowboy who had been riding the Colorado range on horseback since the 1930s.

It was at Fort Carson that Toni married her childhood sweetheart, David. Jerry and I had never been happy about their keeping company, but Toni was very much in love and quite headstrong about it. Fourteen years and two daughters later, they unfortunately, but amicably, divorced.

A year after our arrival at Fort Carson, there was another star for Jerry. Evidently the promotion board felt that he had paid enough penance for his part in the Germany debacle. So now he was now addressed as Major General Curry.

"Kind of good to see a nice guy make it," a fellow general who didn't make the promotion list told him, referring to the commonly held assumption that successful men rise by trampling others underfoot.

23

The Perfect is the Enemy of the Good

"Be thou strong therefore, and shew thyself a man; And keep the charge of the LORD thy God, to walk in his ways, to keep his statutes, and his commandments, and his judgments, and his testimonies."
—I Kings 2:2–3, KJV

From Fort Carson, we moved to Quarters One at Aberdeen Proving Ground, Maryland. It was a large, gray, stone house located across the street from the tennis court and the officers' club. One of the golf greens was situated in our backyard.

Once again I became the First Lady and Jerry became the commanding general, this time of the eleven thousand employees who worked at the Proving Ground. He was in charge of the Army's developmental, engineering, and scientific testing of equipment, putting the "Good Housekeeping Seal of Approval," as it were, on everything from missiles, trucks, tanks, guns, and satellites, down to insulated boots to keep the feet of Eskimo huskies from freezing to the ice under weather conditions encountered by the Arctic troops who used dogsleds.

The command at Aberdeen Proving Ground involved responsibility for some seven million acres of real estate in installations spread throughout the United States, Panama, and Alaska. Many of the men working under Jerry were scientists, with Ph.D.s and other advanced degrees. But he didn't need to be an engineer to inspire and lead men and to be able to manage a large, complex, scientific empire.

It was while we were at Aberdeen that a group of European Christians came to see us in the course of a tour of American Christian organizations and groups. One of our friends from Europe was with them. As they sat around our dining table and prayed before leaving, one said, "Before we go, we want to pray for you, General, and your wife, because we believe that one day you will have even greater influence in this country and around the world."

Months later, I was still digesting all that was said that day. One of the Germans who had prayed for us was an ex-communist who had once fought against all that America stands for, but someone had prayed, and God had saved him and filled him with His Spirit.

For some time I'd not been feeling well, and recently a pain had developed in my lower neck and upper chest area. At first I thought it had something to do with my thyroid, since I had had difficulty with it over the years and part of the time was directed by my doctor to take thyroid medicine. But somehow this pain felt different.

When my doctor at the Aberdeen Proving Ground Hospital examined it, he thought it wise to schedule me for an X-ray. A few weeks later I drove myself over to the hospital and the medical technician took a series of X-rays. After reading them, she asked me to stay in the examining room while she showed them to the doctor.

He later told me that there was cause for concern and that he'd want to prescribe follow-up treatment and would get back to me sometime in the next few days. A few hours after I'd left the hospital, he phoned my husband and asked Jerry to see him that afternoon.

When they met later, he told Jerry that he hadn't told me what he was about to say because he thought he might be misreading the X-rays. But after several other doctors and nurses had looked at them, he was now convinced that his original conclusion had been right and that he was about to phone me and ask me to return for follow-up X-rays. I was suffering from a very aggressive form of cancer that required immediate surgery. The chances of my surviving the surgery were poor and if Jerry and my children had anything that needed to be done or said before the surgery, now was the time to say or do it.

That evening Jerry and I phoned everyone we knew who knew how to pray and asked them to intercede with God for a miracle. We called Jerry's mother, his two brothers, and my brother—all of whom were ordained—as well as many Christian friends. Most of them prayed with us over the phone. We asked them to pray that at the time of surgery, the cancer would be gone from my body.

A few days later Jerry drove me to Walter Reed Army Hospital in Washington, D.C. for emergency surgery. I undressed and put on one of those hospital robes that tie in the back. Jerry put all of my belongings in a suitcase to take home with him.

We said our tearful goodbyes and the surgeons wheeled me off. Before the surgery they were going to take a few more X-rays to see if the cancer had spread. I don't know how long it took, but Jerry said it was about an hour before anyone came back and spoke to him.

"General," the head surgeon said, "our standard procedure is to take final X-rays before surgery to compare with the original X-rays that were used for diagnosis. In that way we can track any progression of the cancer.

"We have good news and bad news for you. The bad news is that somehow someone made a mistake or the film was damaged at the hospital at Aberdeen. Here are the old X-rays and they clearly show a serious cancerous condition. The good news is that the new X-rays show absolutely no cancer."

"Are you telling me that my wife doesn't have cancer, Doctor?"

"That's exactly what I'm telling you. Your wife's body is free and clear of all cancer in any form. When she finishes dressing, you can take her home."

Jerry said his exact words were, "Hallelujah!"

Then came another promotion for Jerry to Deputy Assistant Secretary of Defense for Public Affairs. We were being reassigned back to the Pentagon where Jerry would soon become the Press Secretary to Secretary of Defense Caspar Weinberger. His duties included briefing the national news media and traveling all over the nation and the world explaining the official Department of Defense position "for the record" on matters of every kind.

For the first few months, Jerry stayed in bachelor officers' quarters at Fort Myer during the week. Our youngest daughter Tash, our poodle Leo, our seal point Siamese cat, Princess, and I jammed ourselves and some of the family belongings into a cramped apartment in Bel Air, Maryland, so that Tash could finish her studies and graduate from John Carol High School. Jerry joined us on weekends.

In the middle of all of this confusion and dislocation, son Jerry had enlisted in the Army. "You'd have been proud of your son," Jerry said to me on returning from the Midwest where he had spoken at Butch's basic training graduation. "He's discovered that the perfect is the enemy of the good."

Jerry often used that illustration. At Aberdeen he used to tell his engineers and scientists that, "A workable tank on the battlefield field, all gassed up and ready to go, is infinitely more helpful to men in battle than a colossal design for a tank that is still waiting for perfection on the drawing board. That the tank is practically perfect on paper is not helpful to soldiers who are dying in battle because they don't have tanks."

Similarly, I've learned that life doesn't "wait up" for us to clean out our closets, but has a way of moving inexorably on. If we're to be a part of it, we have to do our living in the now. We can't wait for "someday" when we'll have everything sufficiently "straightened around" according to some idea of perfection.

In 1979, we held a big family reunion in the lush green grass backyard of my parents' home overlooking the Monongahela Valley, where trains thundered by and smoke billowed from steel mills. On the way to the reunion, I had been grieved by the deterioration in what I saw along the way. Familiar streets that had once been bustling with busy people were now trash-littered and nearly deserted. Stores and old houses were boarded up. Bars, billiard rooms, and taverns seemed to be the only places open for business. Barred windows were everywhere—unheard of when I was a child.

Bethlehem Baptist Church still stood in its place, but Jimmy's Restaurant was gone. The concrete stoop that used to lead inside where I could sit spellbound by handsome Jerry Curry now led to the empty ugliness of the dirt and weeds of an unkempt vacant lot. This was the "Rust Belt"—what was left after Big Steel closed its mills.

But there was no grief or disappointment in me at the reunion. The sight of all the delicious food, lovingly prepared, was a foretaste of glory. There were Mom's yeast rolls, light as a feather pillow and big as your fist, and there was Daddy's delicious potato salad, with platters filled with succulent pork chops and crusty fried chicken, bowls of waxy macaroni salad and fresh vegetables, casseroles of Aunt Nellie's incomparable lasagna, gorgeous cakes piled with mountains of icing, pies with melt-in-your-mouth meringue and crusts, soft drinks and iced tea and lemonade. But the food paled in comparison to the fellowship.

My brother George, then a Methodist minister, led off with a prayer of blessing, and we all sang songs of praise to God. When someone started, "Mine eyes have seen the glory of the coming of the Lord," I looked around and saw many misty eyes as we all joined in the vibrant chorus.

There were nearly a hundred of us in all, gathered for the celebration of Independence Day. And what a celebration it was! How much there was to celebrate! Black and brown faces, tan and white together, and all but two or three had become dedicated Christians.

In his prayer of blessing over the food, George thanked God for saving him and his family, for smiling in such a gracious way upon our gathering and for allowing us to meet and enjoy such fellowship in the presence of the Lord. He thanked God for letting us live in a free nation.

When we had eaten, grownups sat in lawn chairs, on picnic benches, or on the steps, while children of all ages—from toddlers to teenagers—sprawled on the grass, propped themselves against the side of the house, or leaned against the convolutions of the trunk of a large old willow tree. When we were all settled, Jerry's brother David, an ordained Baptist minister, preached the good news—that Jesus loves us all and died that we might all be free.

As dusk fell and lights began twinkling like fireflies on the hillsides across the river, we began to sing again, one song following another. My heart cried out that every family in every land could be brought into a relationship with Jesus.

It could happen if only one person in each family would begin to pray, believing. If one family could be brought into the kingdom as ours had been, all families in every city could be brought in. My relationship with God was so precious and wonderful that I wanted everyone to know Him.

Then it was the summer of 1981. Jerry was selected to be the Commanding General of the Military District of Washington. I found myself sitting on the bedroom balcony of our spacious, beautiful colonial brick house that is Quarters Two at Fort McNair, Washington, D.C., watching the riverboats floating serenely past on the lovely Potomac, just a stone's throw away.

Leo, our poodle, who had survived so many moves with us around the world, was stretched out at my feet; and Princess, our friendly Siamese cat, was curled up in my lap. Reflecting on all that had happened since Jerry and I were two little kids in McKeesport, I shook my head and marveled that God could have packed so much life and learning into such a brief span of time.

Perhaps that's why my mind involuntarily started drifting toward thoughts of retirement from military life. When I brought it up one day after a candlelight dinner, I found Jerry more than receptive.

"It's been on my mind a lot these past few months," he said. "Seems to me it's time to move on to something new."

"Have you talked to General Wickham, the Army Chief of Staff, about it?"

"No, John's offered me command of a division but I've turned it down. Two years ago I'd have jumped at it. But it's different now even though command of a division is only offered to a few and is clearly the plum assignment for a Major General.

"I've already had two commands as a Major General, the Army's Test and Evaluation Command at Aberdeen and now the Military District of Washington. A third command, even of a division, won't make me a better Major General."

"Sounds like you're ready to join me in retirement?"

"I think I am, but John has asked me to become Deputy Commander of V Corps in Frankfurt, Germany, our old stomping ground, with the possible command of a corps after that. What do you think?"

"One more tour in Germany might be fun. We started out there and it might be nice to end our military life back there. Besides, I deserve one more overseas shopping trip. Why don't we make it one more for the road?"

"You're on!"

And that's how, once again, we ended up back in Europe.

24

The Rose Bushes

"As I was with Moses, so I will be with thee:
I will not fail thee, nor forsake thee.
Be strong and of a good courage."
—Joshua 1:5-6, KJV

We'd been in Germany nearly a year now and November was ticking off the days, counting down to Thanksgiving. The German weather was typical for Central Europe at this time of year. Damp, gray stratus clouds filtered out all possibility of seeing the sun. The sky was light and somewhere there had to be a sun, but not here, not over Frankfurt.

As usual, I fed Jerry breakfast before he went off to his office in the Abrams building in downtown Frankfurt. Jerry was the V United States Corps Deputy Commander. In addition to his normal duties of helping prepare the corps' tactical units to be prepared to take on and defeat the Russian Army should it cross the border between East and West Germany, he performed mayoral duties for the military communities, such as being superintendent of military children's schools and supervising the local military police who protected our communities.

This particular morning, after Jerry's driver picked him up in his military sedan, I decided to get dressed, and then finish my coffee in front of the TV. The news came on and the announcer essentially said that all was right with the world except that terrorist gangs in Europe such as Baider-Meinhof were "still targeting high ranking officials and generals like—Major General Jerry Curry!" Jerry had gotten used to having a price on his head, but I never did get used to it.

Because of the many years I had spent in Europe before, "foot loose and fancy free," as the saying goes, I found it hard to adjust to the new way of life in Germany. Having to ride in armored cars and always being shadowed by security details and bodyguards was unsettling, no matter how hard I tried to relax and get used to it. Jerry and everyone around him had to carry loaded weapons at all times.

Then, suddenly I remembered that I had promised my next-door neighbor Joan that I would come over to see her this morning. I started to phone her, but since she was right next door I decided to go through the kitchen and slip out the garage door. From there it was only a few feet to her front door.

So out the kitchen door I went, carrying my coffee cup, and pushed the button that raised the garage door. I didn't bother to close either of them because I only would be gone a few minutes.

I rang the bell and Joan answered. She was still in her house-coat and on the phone. She motioned me inside and tried to cut the call short. In a few minutes she had finished. By then I had sat down in a chair at the kitchen table. Though we lived right next door to each other, we hadn't seen each other in about a week.

So we had to catch up on the children, the parties, the shopping and all the other things wives with heavy social calendars do to fulfill their community duties and entertain themselves. Before we knew it, an hour had passed.

And somewhere in the neighborhood there was a problem, because we had heard the wailing of two or three police car sirens—somewhere close.

Finally, our visit was over and Joan poured me a fresh cup of coffee to take home. When I stepped out the front door, I almost collapsed at the sight of German police in their ankle-length coats restraining German shepherd dogs on long leather leashes who were sniffing all around my house. German police cars and U.S. military police cars were blocking all the streets leading up to ours. Soldiers and police were in the process of erecting barricades at the entrances to the housing area.

Of course over the years I'd been party to all sorts of military actions, including living through military coups in third world countries. So while I was a little shocked at the sight of all the activity and while my blood pressure must have shot up considerably, I could still take most things in stride. But what I could not tolerate was the jackbooted German police and their dogs tramping through my rose garden. They had smashed the bushes up so badly that it would probably take years to get them back into decent shape.

And there was Jerry, right in the middle of them. "Why aren't you at work?" I demanded. "Just what is going on here?"

"I'll explain later," he said, climbing back into his sedan.

Evidently after I'd left the house and gone next door, the security alarm had short circuited. During practice alarm drills, we had learned that it actually took the German police less than five minutes to get to the house.

For the rest of the day I fumed. Then toward evening I calmed down and prayed. Finally I felt I knew the will of God. Jerry and I would retire from the Army—now! When Jerry came home I had a delicious dinner prepared to help calm and relax him. Only then would I broach the subject of retiring. If the Lord was really in it, Jerry would agree to retire without offering much resistance.

I worked out my pitch in great detail, "Darling, I've followed you all over the world. I've been both father and mother to your children while you were off killing bad guys in the jungles. Through airplane and helicopter crashes I've never once said that the life you had chosen to live was too dangerous and too nerve-wracking for me, though it was. I've never once complained to you about all the duties I've had to perform as First Lady while you were commanding some military unit. But tonight, I have one small request?" *Yes, that should work out just fine*, I thought.

Besides, I had done all the European shopping I cared to do, including a delicious shopping trip to East Germany through the notorious Checkpoint Charlie in West Berlin. In those days the Berlin Wall was still a formidable barrier, not casually crossed for any purpose, let alone shopping.

Before we turned in that evening, Jerry had agreed to put in for retirement and we sealed the decision with a prayer. Five weeks later, the week before Christmas of 1984, Jerry and I flew back across the Atlantic for the last time.

We left the Army with no retirement plans because we hadn't intended to retire. So we had to make it up as we went along. Both of us were too young and too energetic to hang up our tennis rackets, but we did intend to take a nice, long rest.

So after spending a month with our parents in McKeesport, we booked a flight to the West coast. We debarked at Seattle-Tacoma Airport, rented a car, and meandered south to Puyallup, Washington.

It was so great to see Charlie and Toni again—they and their families lived in Puyallup—we just loved on them and they loved on us. Our four grandchildren (each of our daughters had two daughters) were wonderful to be around. Now we saw how much we'd been missing and how great it was not to have a boss to have to report to. This retirement life wasn't all bad.

Next on the list were my brother-in-law Bob and his wife Joan and their two children. Since the miracle birth, they had adopted a second daughter in Brazil and now lived in Cottage Grove, Oregon.

The phrase "make their home" was a bit of a misnomer. While Cottage Grove is their home base, Bob spends about a third of his time in Finland where he conducts Christian seminars, teaches college-level Bible courses, and travels the country as a sort of an itinerant missionary. He also spends a lot of time ministering the gospel in Estonia, Latvia, Lithuania, and Russia. The other third of his time he spends traveling around Brazil encouraging Christian churches and ministries.

Bob happened to be home when we phoned to ask if we could visit, just a few days before we hoped to arrive. We had never seen their two daughters, and it was a real treat to be able to listen to their tales about living in Brazil for so many years. Both of them had dual Brazilian and American citizenship. Years later, Bob's whole family was able to return to Brazil with him to live for a few years.

We dragged out the visit for as long as we could, and then climbed back into our rental car and headed south. This time it was to Grant's Pass, Oregon, where Dr. Dave and Kathy Oehling were part of the Grant's Pass medical community. Dave was a general surgeon and Kathy taught nursing at the local college.

Many years before, when Jerry had been a battalion commander in Schweinfurt, Germany, Captain Oehling had been his battalion surgeon. We became close friends and now, twenty-five years later, we were still in contact.

After a few days in Grant's Pass, we had to let the Oehilings get on with their lives. So after a prayer, we struck out toward Chico and Sally Holiday's ranch in northern California. They needed a lot of cheering up because just a few nights before, cattle rustlers had raided their herd, carrying off some of their best cows. In the early hours of the morning they had arrived with eighteen wheelers, cut their way through the barbed wire fences, loaded the cattle up in the trucks, and driven off. They were never caught.

From the Holidays we again meandered south, visiting friends and relatives from Sacramento to San Francisco and all points in between. What a delight it was to get reacquainted with the West Coast of the good old United States of America.

Too soon it was time to board another flight and point our noses east. Washington, D.C. was our destination. Our christian friends Admiral and Mrs. Burkhardt had extended an invitation to us to stay with them for an indeterminate period of time, until we could figure out what God wanted us to do with our lives.

Fortunately they had an old detached servants' cabin in back of the main house where we could stack our suitcases and ourselves and still be out of their way. Barbara undertook to pray daily with us about our circumstances. When we departed she gave me small antique brass chest. She said the chest represented God's promise that one day I would live in a house filled with treasures. Larry, a submariner, was still on active duty and under the pressures all senior officers experience while working in the military's Washington headquarters.

One day the phone in our cabin rang and a voice said, "Please hold for Pat Robertson." Over the years Jerry and I had shaken hands with Pat and his wife Dee-Dee a few times, but we had never exchanged more than a few words and did not feel that we really knew him, nor he us.

Pat had founded the Christian Broadcasting Network, or CBN, in Virginia Beach as well as Regent College. His flagship TV program, the 700 Club, was well-known nationally, as were many of his charity projects.

Jerry took the phone from me, and he and Pat talked for about ten minutes. Pat had decided to found a public policy "think tank" and he wanted to know if Jerry would head up the effort.

Jerry promised to pray about it. Pat said he would be in town in few weeks and would like to meet.

A month later Pat welcomed us to CBN and Virginia Beach. We found that he had assembled a group of first-class people. They were bright, energetic, strong Christians, and just plain good Americans.

Shortly after we arrived, we learned that Pat had decided to run for president of the United States. This news caught us completely off guard, undoubtedly because we had only been back from Germany a short time. We had no idea that Pat had political aspirations, though thinking back, we were not surprised because Pat's father had been a U.S. congressman and senator.

It turns out that Pat had asked Jerry to come to Virginia Beach, in part, to help him with his campaign. So wanting to oblige, Jerry agreed to do some legwork putting together an exploratory campaign organization.

Once Pat and Jerry started working more closely together it became obvious that they did not see eye-to-eye. As much as we love Pat, we didn't always agree politically. But Jerry had made a commitment to start the think tank and if part of that job meant helping his boss put together a campaign, then he would do the best he could. Over the next few months, as time allowed, he put together the framework for what would later be called the "Robertson for President" campaign.

Then, as often happens, something widened the growing rift between the two men.

Jerry and Pat had flown to Houston, where Pat had been invited to be the keynote speaker to the Christian Oilmen's Association. When the oilmen learned that Jerry was coming with Pat, they asked if he would be willing to speak to them as the final conference speaker.

On the flight back to Virginia Beach, Pat asked Ben Kinchelow, his co-host on the 700 Club, how his speech had gone over with the oilmen.

"It was a great speech," Ben told him. "But the speech that impressed the oilmen most was the one given by Jerry. Some of them said that they thought Jerry was the one who should be running for president." Ben is guileless and meant no harm, but his remarks killed the possibility of Pat and Jerry ever working together.

Several months later, Jerry resigned from his position as president of the think tank. The think tank was fully operational and Pat's national election campaign organization had been solidly established. Regrettably, Jerry and Pat had established a mutual admiration society in which Pat didn't think very highly of Jerry, and Jerry didn't think very highly of Pat.

25

Chateau Antioch

"See, I am sending my angel before you to lead
you safely to the land I have prepared for you.
Pay attention to him, and obey all of his instructions."
–Exodus 23:20, NLT

Jerry took a job as Vice President for Business Development of a computer systems integration company located in Norfolk, Virginia. For a year he worked hard and things went well, and then he was called upon by some politicians of the Virginia State Republican Party.

They were looking for someone to run against a Democratic incumbent for Virginia's Second Congressional District which was then composed of the cities of Norfolk and Virginia Beach. Without hesitation Jerry said, "No." For months they kept phoning, but Jerry never wavered in his answer.

I thought there was a spiritual problem with his "No." So, being a good helpmate, one day I helped him get some clarity.

"Jerry," I began. "Have you prayed about running for congress?"

"No," he said. "I know that God doesn't want me to run for congress."

"How do you know that unless you've prayed about it?"

"I just know it deep down in my gut."

"Well," I said softly, "we've always prayed about things like this and you've never made a major decision concerning our lives without consulting me. This is a major decision, and you haven't asked me for my opinion."

Jerry looked a little less sure of himself. "Well, I just assumed you felt the same way about it as I did."

"Maybe I do and maybe I don't, but I want you to really pray about it before we discuss it."

"Fair enough," he muttered.

The next morning at breakfast he brought up the subject in a subdued voice. "How do you feel about me running for congress?" he asked.

"I think the Lord wants you to run," I said, munching on my whole-grain toast.

"So do I," he said, sounding grim. "I've prayed about it and much to my chagrin, something inside says that I should run. But I only know one way to do this. I'm running to win."

That's how it came about in early 1988, that the "Curry for Congress" campaign was born. It turned out to be a three-man race: the incumbent, Jerry, and a Republican independent who siphoned off votes from Jerry.

The first major event was scheduled and Jerry asked me to be ready at 6:30 P.M. I had to tell him that I wasn't going to be campaigning with him.

"Why not?" he complained. "You are the one who got me into this."

"Yes, I know, honey," I said. "But God told me that you were to run, not that you were going to win. And besides, I'm not keen to be a congressman's wife, with all that that entails."

I did appear with Jerry at a few events, like a barbecue or a "pig pullen." And I did give several speeches, but mostly I let Jerry and his young assistants knock on doors and ask people to vote for Jerry. Our daughter, Natasha, drove up from Dallas and worked for him during the entire campaign. Toni and Charlie flew in from Washington State a few days before the election and worked the polls on Election Day.

One day Jerry returned home, tired and hot from campaigning door-to-door, and related a humorous story. When he approached one particular house he saw a large sign over the door. It read, "This house protected by a pit bull with AIDS."

Even though my heart was not in it, still I went to the election-night soirée and stood by my man as he was slaughtered. Jerry had worked hard, but knocking off a congressional incumbent is not easy. He lost.

President Bush, Sr. offered Jerry a job in his new Administration, and in late March he became a full-time consultant to the Department of Transportation as Administrator Designate, working in the National Highway Traffic Safety Administration (NHTSA). In the fall, Jerry was unanimously confirmed by the Senate. I held the Bible when he took the oath of office.

As always, Jerry worked hard and his work went well. A few years after he had left the Administration, the *Automotive News Magazine*, which is the motor vehicle manufacturing industry's trade newspaper, covered the 25th anniversary of NHTSA. Both the editorial staff and the government employees of NHTSA said that Jerry was the best administrator the agency had ever had.

Early on in his tour as administrator, Jerry's father became stricken with bone cancer. Most weekends found us driving up to the Pittsburgh area to see him.

He had entered the hospital to have his prostate treated and for some reason they had decided to give him a body scan. He lit up the screens. The doctors said it was the worst case of bone cancer they had ever seen.

Even in death, he remained his difficult, crusty self. After the doctors had a bedside conference with him and described the various treatments they could give him to prolong his life, he wouldn't consent to any of them.

He asked for, and got, a packet of pain killers. Then he discharged himself from the hospital and drove himself home. A year later he died in excruciating pain.

Meanwhile, Jerry and I had joined St. George's Episcopal Church near our townhouse in Arlington. We both sang in the choir and joined the local Bible study and intercessory prayer group. The congregation was comprised of many wonderful families and we loved to worship alongside them.

We were also active in the community and I was appointed a member of the Arlington County Arts Council. We met once a month to allocate community funds to various artistic groups and artists such as painters and poets.

At the same time, Jerry and I needed to make some long-range plans as to where we wanted to live for the rest of our lives. Many of our military friends had elected to make Arizona their home after leaving the Army. So we took a flight out to Arizona, rented a car, and crisscrossed the state looking for a place to settle.

We found several places that attracted us greatly, but in the end decided to put down our roots in Virginia. Though Jerry had been born in Pennsylvania, both his parents and their parents had been born in the Shenandoah River Valley, south of Lexington, Virginia. So when, after much prayer, we decided to become Virginians, it seemed the natural thing to do.

Of course this meant that we'd have to leave the townhouse in Alexandria. Running up and down three flights of stairs all day was a bit much. As in all things, God solved this problem for us.

One Sunday afternoon Jerry, who was looking through the Washington Post newspaper, said to me, "Here's a model house I'd like to look at."

I looked at the ad. The model was located in Warrenton, Virginia. For purposes of commuting into Washington, D.C., it was like living on the backside of the moon. "That's much too far out," I complained.

"Well, if you weren't here, I'd go alone. So, if you don't mind, I'll drive out to see it by myself."

"Not without me," I shouted, running back to the bedroom to get dressed.

We liked the model, but felt it wasn't very imaginative, and it was a bit pricey. The builder was desperate to open a new section of land for development where no houses had been built. He wanted to use us to open up the new area.

So he assured us that he could make any changes we wanted, or, if we wanted him to, come up with an entirely new design. For that much money I was certain he would do whatever we wanted. In the end, we chose to make substantial changes to a new design for which he had previously drawn up plans, but had never built a house from.

After several weeks and many conversations we came into agreement and one day found ourselves at the bank talking about construction loans. Since the money was more than we wanted to pay, and since by this time Jerry was out of the government and didn't have a real job, we prayed that if this house wasn't the Lord's will, the bank would refuse to give us the construction loan.

When the banker had finished going over all the paperwork with us, the moment of truth we had been praying about came. The banker looked at Jerry and said, "Mr. Curry, what kind of work do you do?"

Jerry looked him straight in the eye and without either blinking or laughing out loud said, "I'm a business consultant." This was code for, "I don't have a job"—at least that's how it was with us.

Without a pause the banker said, "Your loan is approved."

As we walked out of the bank Jerry mumbled, "Now what am I going to do? I was counting on the loan being turned down. Now I don't have any excuse not to build the house."

This put us in possession of ten acres of land on top of the southern slope of Bull Run Mountain, in the northwest corner of Prince William County. The nearest town was called Haymarket.

To be closer to the construction site, we moved to Delaplane, Virginia, into the country house of some friends, Robin and Susan Anderson. They put up with us for several months and we grew to love their cat, Ariadne.

From the time when the first dirt was dug out of the earth, signaling the beginning of the foundation, until the last piece of furniture was put in place, it was obvious that the hand of God was with us in the construction of our new home. It reminded us of the directions God had given King David to build the temple. No, this was no temple; it was just that everything seemed to wonderfully fit into place. Barbara Burkhardt was right; it was a house filled with treasures.

To make this happen, God provided Daryl Bates, the designer to coordinate everything. His father Ray and mother Toots were old family friends who had designed and supervised the furnishing of residences all over the world, including the King's palace in Morocco. When we had lived at Fort McNair in Washington, D.C., they had come in and arranged our home so we could instantly start entertaining guests, from the Secretary of Defense to the President of Costa Rica.

We wanted a home that felt comfortable and lived-in, and that's exactly what Daryl gave us. But it was the miraculous touches that made the difference. For example, a blue and white Wedgwood vase that Jerry had bought me for a birthday present many years before when we were living in Germany fit perfectly with the window treatments even though Daryl had chosen them without ever seeing the vase.

Months after we had moved into the house, we got around to unpacking my fine European china and found that the peacocks in the two large paintings on the dining room wall matched the Kutani Crane pattern, and the same colors happened to be in the rug under the dining room table.

I had never liked the idea of dining room china cabinets because they require so much precious space in the average-size dining room and make it crowded to have large, sit-down dinners. So I asked Daryl to recess two large, mirror-covered closets into the dining room walls for me. He covered the face of the closets with two ornate mirrors, the frames of which he carved to compliment our family history.

Daryl took Jerry and me to New York for several shopping trips, by train. The result was that we now enjoy living in one of the most beautifully decorated homes we have ever had. Daryl Bates was truly a God-send.

Here's another example: Daryl wanted to hang a large painting in the great room but there was no place for it. So he built a faux wall between the Great Room and the Morning Room just to display a large painting. It is a hundred-year-old copy of the painting *The Storm* by Cot, and depicts a young girl and boy running away from a storm while trying to protect their heads from the rain by a large scarf. The painting reminds me of our childhood when Jerry and I used to run and play in the woods.

Jerry had seen an engraving on the wall of the Fort Myer Officers' Club, titled *Washington and His Generals*, which he wanted for the dining room. Daryl contacted the manager of the club and persuaded him to go back into the club's retired files and try to find the original bill of sale. After much searching he found it.

It turned out that the engraving had been purchased from a store in Baltimore about the year 1900. Daryl called information and found out that the store was still in existence and still doing business. He visited them and found that the plate hadn't been used in years, but might be stored in the cellar. Sure enough, a search located it and they were kind enough to run off the engraving which now graces our dining room wall along with two paintings of peacocks. How I got the peacock paintings is another story.

The house is deliberately designed to have a European feel and old-world charm, complete with the crystal chandeliers Jerry and I had dreamed of as children in our dates at the ice cream parlor in McKeesport. Daryl has carried on that theme throughout. We named our house "Chateau Antioch" because of the European feel and because the house is near Antioch Road, and the little, historical Antioch Church. In the Book of Acts, the followers of Christ were first called Christians in Antioch.

At the Chateau Antioch, we live high up on our mountain in splendid solitude. Daily we are visited by herds of deer, clusters of rabbits, fox, wild turkeys, groundhogs, and a menagerie of birds. From time to time I reflect over the years of my life and wonder what it all means and what the future holds. My Lord does nothing by accident. He has deliberately blessed us far beyond what we could ask or think.

Early on I learned that God has a plan for each of our lives. Some may choose not to believe in God, and so miss what He has for them. But for those who believe and seek His guidance, He is ever present and willing to walk alongside, helping and guiding. Our job, with His help, is to find the right path and to stay on it.

Each of us has God-given gifts and talents. Our job is to recognize them and seek to nurture and develop them to the best of our abilities. This falls in line with our trying to be the best people we can possibly be and trying to contribute as much as we can to our country, family, friends, and communities.

Attitude is everything. As a newly married young lady of seventeen, I left home determined to do well in life. And I determined to look to older, successful people, especially Christians, for wisdom and guidance. I knew there would be many hard things ahead for me, but believed that there was nothing God, Jerry and I couldn't jointly handle. And that is how it has been.

I have always loved people, and loved to help others, and have tried hard to pass on what little wisdom I may have gleaned from life and from observing others who successfully came to grips with life's challenges. For the most part, people have returned that love. Daily I pray for others that God will help them and meet their needs just as he meets mine and Jerry's. Still, there are a few who will not let you love them no matter how hard you try.

But the most important thing has been and will always be my personal relationship to Jesus, the Son of God. That is my core, my foundation. I understand that there are others who either believe differently from me or not at all, and I respect their God-given right to go their own way. But for me the essence of who I am is whose I am.

It is important to know who you are and what you stand for, and to act in character. I try to start each day with prayer and then pray my way through whatever God has in store for me. In that way, the rest of the day becomes whatever God allows. So long as I stay in close contact with Him, nothing is going to come along that God can't handle. There is an old hymn that often comes to mind which sums up my feelings. Its words are, "God is my refuge and strength, a very present help in trouble."

In addition to loving God, my life has always been wrapped around the drive and desire to help others and to make a difference. When I share my thoughts with others I try to put them first and not dominate the conversation, because they have thoughts too, and their thoughts are important to them. Being attentive to others and listening to what they say has always made a difference in my life.

When I make wrong decisions, and at times we all do, I try to learn from them and to develop strategies not to repeat them. We'll never be perfect, but we can strive to be decent and honest and to help others along the way.

The result is, I've learned to prayerfully turn my principles and standards into habits. That way I don't have to think about what's right or wrong, good or bad, smart or stupid. Life just flows naturally. In every situation, God either has already prepared me for what it is I need to do or say, or a still, small voice deep inside speaks a word of wisdom to my mind as I need it—even when I'm caught off-guard.

Once upon a time Jerry and I were two little kids living, playing, and growing up in a small town in western Pennsylvania, singing together in the church choir. We had been taught to live our lives respectfully and civilly, with courtesy and dignity. Jerry's father was a steelworker and my father was a coal miner. Jerry had proposed to me when I was ten and he was thirteen. I accepted.

Then along came the Korean War and Jerry enlisted as a Private to fight for our country. Two years later he was a Second Lieutenant of Infantry, and we were married. Thirty years later he had worked his way up through the ranks to Major General. On three continents I have worked alongside him, being his helper, friend, confidant and lover. I still am, after more than fifty years of marriage. Perhaps this is why some say that I am truly, "The General's Lady."

Major General Jerry R. Curry

FROM PRIVATE TO GENERAL
An African American Soldier
Rises Through the Ranks

Major General Jerry Curry vividly describes his life journey of military missions, powerful positions, and his relationship with the true source of authority—his Father in heaven.

Fern C. Willner

WHEN FAITH IS ENOUGH
A Safari of Destiny that Reveals
Principles to Live By

A faith-inspiring story of a missionary wife and mother of seven relying completely on God in the heart of Africa. *Accompanying workbook also available for discussion groups in 2007*

Rev. Samuel Doctorian
with Elizabeth Moll Stalcup, Ph.D.

GOD WILL NOT FAIL YOU
A Life of Miracles in the Middle East
and Beyond

The miraculous life story of Rev. Samuel Doctorian, the renowned evangelist used mightily by God in the Middle East and around the world.